# THE WISDOM OF MAN

Selected Discourses
by
M. R. Bawa Muhaiyaddeen

THE FELLOWSHIP PRESS
Philadelphia, PA

*Library of Congress Cataloging in Publication Data*

MUHAIYADDEEN, M. R. BAWA.
   The wisdom of man.

   1. Sufism.   I. Title.
BP189.M7      297'.4      80-20541

**Hard Cover**  ISBN 0-914390-16-3
**Soft Cover**  ISBN 0-914390-45-7

Copyright © 1983
by the Bawa Muhaiyaddeen Fellowship
5820 Overbrook Ave., Philadelphia, PA 19131
All rights reserved. No portion of this book
may be reproduced in any manner without
written permission from the publisher.

Printed in the United States of America
by THE FELLOWSHIP PRESS
Bawa Muhaiyaddeen Fellowship

First Printing: 1980
Second Printing: 1983
Third Printing: 1994

# Acknowledgements

The discourses presented here were spoken by M. R. Bawa Muhaiyaddeen in Philadelphia during 1979. They were given in Tamil, an ancient Dravidian language found in parts of India and Sri Lanka, and translated into English by Professor Ajwad Macan-Markar, Dr. M. Z. Markar, Dr. K. Ganesan, and Mrs. Crisi Beutler.

This publication also includes three works of art, or heart's work as the artist calls them, designed and drawn by Bawa Muhaiyaddeen. In the insignia on the half-title page, the Arabic lettering reads, "In the name of God, the Most Merciful, the Most Gracious." This is an invocation respectfully spoken before any undertaking. Next, on page four is a painting of two parrots representing mind and desire sitting on the tree of life. On page twenty-eight is a reproduction of a light box which was etched on the back of a mirror, painted, and illuminated from behind. The Arabic words from top to bottom are Allah, Muhammad, and Muhaiyaddeen. Encircled below are the three Arabic letters, *alif*, *lām*, and *mīm*.

# Contents

| | |
|---|---:|
| INTRODUCTION | 1 |
| A BENEFIT TO ALL | 3 |
| THE LIGHT OF THE PROPHETS | 27 |
| THE WORLD WITHIN AND WITHOUT | 51 |
| THREE QUESTIONS | 87 |
| GLOSSARY | 139 |
| INDEX | 159 |

Wisdom is the light to guide your life,
    faith is the path, truth is God,
    and understanding this is peace.

*M. R. Bawa Muhaiyaddeen*

# Introduction

This is a collection of four discourses spontaneously spoken by M. R. Bawa Muhaiyaddeen. Since 1971 he has periodically visited the United States, sharing freely his love for God and his compassion for all lives. Never seeking personal gain or honors, he constantly gives of his love and wisdom. This book is such a gift.

Each talk is rich with wisdom and clarity. The first, "A Benefit to All," describes the exalted qualities with which we should conduct our lives. The second, "The Light of the Prophets," speaks of our relationship with the prophets who brought the word of God–not the historical connection, but rather the living, unchanging, unending connection in our hearts. The third talk is entitled "The World Within and Without." Mankind has spent centuries exploring the world which surrounds him, but within him lies another universe, a mirror reflection of everything he perceives outside himself. This chapter explores that inner world. The fourth discourse,

"Three Questions," is a letter written in response to a recent television series about the world's religions. On one program, the commentator stated that for thirty years he had been asking three questions. "Who am I? Why am I here? and Who is God?" In this letter, M. R. Bawa Muhaiyaddeen shares the answers reached through his own search.

Together these four talks explain many of the fundamental soul-searching questions we all encounter. To understand the answers is the wisdom of man. While reading this book, you will soon recognize that the words spoken here are not the usual rhetoric or intellectual explanations we normally hear but come from the experience of a living, authentic holy man. We all need to learn from such experience. We need this clarity and understanding to stabilize us in this rapidly changing world. So open this book and open the world within you. Know the wisdom of man and you will know the purpose of your life. Read, reflect, and understand. May God help us. Amen.

# A Benefit to All

*Bismillāhir-Rahmānir-Rahīm:* In the name of God, the Most Gracious, the Most Merciful.

O God, please grant us the wealth of the three worlds, the world of souls, this world, and the next world. Please bestow these three worlds upon us and grant us Your grace. Amen.

May You take away from us everything other than You and everything that has been made in comparison to You, and may You grant us Your grace. Amen.

O the One who has no equal, the One who has no destruction, the One who is undiminishing, O Allah who is the plenitude and who is all-pervading, the One who has all the understanding, the One who is the resplendence in the heart, the One who is that light within *īmān*, or absolute faith, the Perfect One who fills our heart with the plenitude of love, please grant us Your qualities, Your actions, Your grace, and Your treasure. Amen.

Remove all the aspects of the world that are within us and fill us with the aspect of the next world. Remove from us the darkness of this physical world, and grant us that light which is the next world. You exist as the light, so please grant us that light by which we can dispel the darkness of the world. Amen.

My Limitless One of Grace, may You grant us all the immeasurable wealth that You have with You. O the One who has no darkness, the One who has no torpor, the One who has no desire, the One who has no attachments, the One who has no connection to the world, the One who has no equal or comparison, that Power who rules everything, may You grant us Your gracious attributes. Amen. Amen. Amen.

My very precious children, my jeweled lights, my own born children who are my rightful ones, my children who are the light within my heart, those who are born with me, who are the light of my eyes, my loving children who are the love of my wisdom, my children who are born with me as six lives but exist as one life, who are a part of my body and my wisdom and my *imān*, children who are intermingled in my love, my very precious children, may God protect you and me, and may He sustain us. Amen. My love to all of you.

My very precious children, my jeweled lights, there is a resonance known as *Allāhu*. And from within this resonance which is within the innermost heart, or *qalb*, comes the explanation. And within that explanation is that vibration which vibrates within our lives. And within that vibration is that plenitude of light which exists within us. We should strive to reach that plenitude.

My very precious children, my jeweled lights, look at all the things around us. Each creation benefits us in some way, does it not? Take the grass, for example. It is useful to the cows and the bulls and the goats. Look at a tree; it benefits so many. Some trees bear fruit for you to eat, and those that don't bear fruit give shade, do they not? The fruits, the shrubs, and the flowers are beneficial to others. A flower can give you a sweet fragrance, and the water from a pond can quench your thirst. The sun gives us light, the moon gives coolness, and the stars also give their light. In all God's creation everything benefits some life or other. Each creation helps and provides comfort for other lives.

My very precious children, you must realize this. The shrubs, the trees, the flowers, the grass, the rains, and the clouds all give us comfort. If they can comfort us, then shouldn't we also be able to comfort others? We, too, must come to benefit others. We must become beneficial to all other lives.

If a man sits by the side of a mountain, the shade from the mountain provides coolness and prevents the heat of the sun from falling upon him. Similarly, if you become a good person, then you will be able to comfort other lives that are in danger, and you will be able to provide peace in time of heated difficulties. If we are virtuous and good and selfless, then we will be like the mountain which serves without expecting any reward or praise in return. If we can be in that state and give peace to other lives, then we will be of benefit to others.

A tree shades us from the heat of the sun and protects us from the winds and rain. A tree can be of such great help. It bears fruits for others to eat, but the tree never eats the fruit that it bears, does it? So, like that, even if we live in this world, we shouldn't have the thought that we are enjoying the pleasures of the world. We must be like the tree which bears fruits but never partakes of them.

Similarly, although many lives exist within the water, the water never eats any of those lives. Instead, it gives of itself to others. For example, there are many grasses that are found in the water, but the water doesn't eat that grass. It gives it all to other lives. Like that, my very precious children, if we are to exist as true human beings, then we should be helpers to all other lives. We should not look to satisfy our own comfort and our own hunger. We should not look for praise and honors. We should not look for any of these. We must at least perform the duty of the grass and shrubs.

God does duty without any selfishness or attachment, and He feeds all lives. Is it not so? We should be in the same state as God. My very precious children, my jeweled lights, it is time that we lose ourselves and understand our Leader.

A flower gives its sweet fragrance, does it not? Like the flower that blooms and gives its fragrance, our heart must bloom and that wisdom must come. Only when that wisdom blooms will the flower of the heart blossom. And only when that love blooms within the heart will that fragrance come from within you. Should not our hearts blossom like the flower so that we, too, can give that fragrance? All lives will pay obeisance to that fragrance; all will respect that fragrance.

A flower doesn't need to advertise itself saying, "I am a flower." Others will be aware of its fragrance, and they will be attracted and drawn toward it. So if a mere flower can do that, then when we exist with a flowering and blossoming heart, and when we have that fragrance in our heart, those who love God and have faith in God will come near us. Children, jeweled lights of my eyes, just as a flower attracts others, this heart will attract those who have faith in God. We should be in that state.

If we pluck a flower and remove it from the tree, it will shrivel up and lose its fragrance. The flower can give its fragrance only as long as it is on the tree. Similarly, if we leave our correct state, that flower within the innermost heart will fade. We must remain connected to the tree which is the heart. If we leave the heart behind, then the flower in our heart will perish. This is what will happen if we go in search of praise and honors and positions for the sake of our pride. Then we will be like the flower that was plucked from the tree; all the good that we have will dry up within us. Is it not so?

Every one of my children, please think about this. God always exists in the same place, and He does His duty without praise, without honors, and without the ego of the 'I'. Such is His duty. This is how we should try to perform our duty, our prayers, our devotions, and our worship. There is no God worthy of worship other than the Almighty God, *Allāhu ta'ālā*.

My precious children, you must think. You must reflect. You must realize. You must know. And you must understand. What must we understand? That Allah exists everywhere. That Allah exists in all lives and understands all lives. The One who exists everywhere, does He not exist within us? Do we have to go in search of Him? Do we have to recite a mantra to draw Him within us? Do we have to perform some *tantra* or trick? Do we have to display a miracle to see Him? Do we have to fly to the skies to see Him? Do we have to close our eyes and wait to see Him?

My precious children, my jeweled lights, see how the water falls when it rains. It goes to all places and gives benefit to each. When it rains, you will see the trees and the grass and all things become bright; everything has that coolness within it. The ponds become filled, and the excess water drains into the ocean. How beautiful it is when that water runs to the ocean. When the rain falls to the earth and the pond, it is of benefit to all living creatures, is it not?

Similarly, with every breath our heart should glorify God. At all times, we must allow the rain of God's grace to fall. Every minute, every second, with every breath, we must glorify Him. In every second we must have the intention of worshiping Him. Every word that we speak must be His word. Every thought must be His thought. This must be our state. In our thoughts, in our breath, in our speech, and in our intentions, we should be communicating with God. We should live in His intention. Whatever duty we may do, He must always be in our intention.

This is not a very big thing, my precious children. We think it is a very big weight to carry. But look at the breath: whatever work we may be doing, that breath goes on working automatically, does it not? When we are working, does the breath stop working? When we work, do our eyes stop functioning? They still function, do they not? Whatever work we may do, doesn't the blood keep on circulating? Does it stop circulating because we are busy working? No, it does not. Whenever we do anything, our breath always flows continuously. Our chest moves in and out, every piece of flesh twitches, every hair follicle rises up, and all the pores of the skin remain open all the time. If these things can always perform their functions, then can we not always have our intention on God?

Our intention and our faith in God must always be with us, just as our breath moves continuously. Our *īmān* must be constant. Those thoughts, that intention of God, that breath, that speech, that look, and that sound should operate continuously as do the automatic functions of the body. That is what is called *Dhikr*, the remembrance of God. If you always intend God just as the functions always work inside your body, then that is what is called worship or prayer.

This is not a very heavy burden to carry. Everything else works automatically; if this too can work automatically, then it is called grace, God's *rahmat*. It is that grace that we must spread to all. Like the rain which gives so much comfort and coolness, we should quench the thirst of others. We should satisfy the hunger of others and try to comfort their tiredness. These are the duties that we must perform.

My children, we should never say, "This is difficult, that is difficult," or "This is impossible." It is what we carry within us that is really heavy. When it rains and there are floods, you can see trees and boats floating away in the water. But when you try to lift a tree from the earth, it is very heavy. If we try to carry a tree ourselves, it is very heavy. Similarly, if you try to carry a ship, it is very heavy. But when the ship is on the water, is it heavy then? No, it is not heavy for the water. Once we put the ship in the water, what happens? We can load it with seventy times its own weight and still it is not too much weight for the water.

My very precious children, all the weights and heavy things that we have collected during our life are like this. We try to carry them with us. We try to carry the earth, we try to carry the air, we carry our desires, and we carry our attachments and our love for our relations. These things are heavy because we are carrying them against the gravity of the earth.

But if you can let each breath carry the vibration of *Lā ilāha, ill-Allāhu*—There is no God but

God, and only God exists; if you can take all this weight and hand it over to that *Hu, ill-Allāhu*, it is like handing over all those weights to the ship. Then you will have no weight. You will have no burdens to carry. Just as the water was able to support the ship, Allah will carry all your burdens. They are not heavy to Him, just as the ship and its cargo are not heavy to the water. If you surrender to God in that state, there is no weight or burden for you at all; *Allāhu* will carry all those burdens. But if you just give half to the water and you attempt to carry the other half, how can you bear that? How can you carry that?

My precious children, please reflect on this. Only when you give the boat entirely to the water can the water carry it. Then no matter what you may load on it, the water can still carry it. Like that, we must give our burdens entirely to God, and say, *"La ilāha,* There is no God but God, *ill-Allāhu,* Only You exist, O God." And that One who is the benevolence of all the universes, the *Rahmatul-'ālamīn,* will carry all our burdens and all our weight. The more weight you give Him, the more He will carry.

If you reflect on this, you will realize that if we can live in this state of surrender to God, then we will have no fear or difficulties whatsoever. Then it becomes very easy to worship God. The difficulty lies in trying to carry things away from the earth and in trying to surrender these burdens to Allah. There are always the blood attachments, races, and religions that pull us. We carry them with us, and that is what gives us this weight. But if we can take this weight and surrender it to God, then worship becomes very easy, to reach God becomes easy, to speak to Him becomes easy, to receive His benevolence is easy, to merge with Him is easy, and to reach His kingdom is easy. We must think about this. My very precious children, each one of you must think this over. We must reflect on each and every thing.

Look at all the things that are surrounding us. Study them. Try to reflect and understand. Let us look around and see. God created each one of His creations, and He gave them the appropriate levels of wisdom and understanding. These creations are like books to us; within each one there is an explanation. If we can understand that explanation, then we can understand the truth, can we not?

Everything that we see is visible. Everything

has a history. Everything moves and grows. Everything has a sound. Everything speaks. Everything has a smell. Everything has actions and qualities. Everything has a benefit and a use. Let us reflect on this. These are lessons for us to learn, are they not? And we can try to digest these lessons, can we not?

It is the same within our body. Within this body, we have a huge universe. What we are seeing outside is just a small world. It is just a tiny point, a dot. But there is a universe within us, and within that are the 18,000 universes, and within those are millions and millions of creations. We must see all of these. We must look after them. We must bring them into some state of usefulness, and we must teach them. We must teach them justice. We must judge them. We must preach to them. We must teach them wisdom. We must give them the light of the soul. We need to instruct them in so many things. This is the court of judgment and justice. As we become realized beings or *Insān-Kāmil*, we will become the chief justice in that court of justice.

We are the ones who have analytic wisdom. All the creatures that are within us have only the first three levels of consciousness. They have feeling, awareness, and intellect. Beyond these three levels, we have evaluation, subtle wisdom, divine analytic wisdom (the wisdom of the *qutbiyat* or the wisdom which explains), and divine luminous wisdom (the wisdom of the *Nūr*, the resplendence of God). Using these faculties of wisdom, we must become true human beings so we can rule and guide these creatures that are within us.

There have been 124,000 prophets, *qutbs*, saints, and lights of God who have come to this world. Of these, 25 prophets were selected. They were shepherds; they looked after cattle, goats, camels, and horses. Why did the prophets have to become shepherds to animals like cows and goats, horses and camels, donkeys and asses? We must think about this.

*We* are those camels and goats and bulls and horses. Within us there are so many animals, and it was to shepherd those animals that the prophets came. We were the cows and goats and camels to the prophets. They came to shepherd us and to make us into men.

We must understand that it is we whom they shepherded. Did they really shepherd the camels or the goats or the cows? Whom did they shepherd really? We were in that animal state, and we are the ones who were shepherded. The prophets performed the work of a shepherd as an example to demonstrate what they were really doing. They were trying to shepherd us and make us true men.

Once we become true human beings, then we, too, must shepherd these goats and cows—not the cows and goats which exist outside, but the ones within us. We have a huge world within us, and those creatures exist there in the form of shadows. They exist in the form of demons and ghosts; they exist as foxes and dogs, rats and cats. Each of them attacks and destroys the other. One kills and tortures the other; one drinks the blood of the other. The viruses and germs, the thoughts, demons, and satans, all devour each other. All the tigers and bears and dogs and cats and snakes and scorpions and all the things that exist in hell are within us. Just as the prophets shepherded us, we have to shepherd those things which exist in our inner world. We have to shepherd everything that exists in that huge universe within us.

In order to do this, we have the whip of $īmān$ and the staff of faith, certitude, and determination. In order to cross this dense jungle, we have to hold onto that staff, have that whip in our hand, and carry the torch of wisdom. With the light of wisdom, the whip of *īmān*, and the staff of faith, certitude, and determination, we must try to shepherd those animals within us. Once we can herd those animals, then we must give judgment according to their merit.

When we recognize what we are bringing up, we will realize the justice of 'Umar 'ibnul-Khattāb, companion of the Prophet and second caliph of Islam, may Allah be pleased with him. Look at his judgment and his sense of justice. Read about his justice and the judgments that he delivered during his time. That is the kind of justice and judgment that we must perform in this world of ours. If we have that justice within us, and if we can give judgment to each of those lives within us, then we, too, can become such a leader.

If we act according to that state of justice and judgment, and if we have that state of truthfulness, we will find that even the mongoose and the cobra will be able to live together. We will find that tigers and goats will live together. The lion and the bull will live together. The small and the large fish will live together. They will all be able to live in the same place. Things that are inimical to each other will live in a perfect state of harmony in the kingdom of justice.

If we have that state of justice within us, and if we can perform that true judgment, then Allah is within us all the time. That judgment is within us. All lives are within us. The love for all lives is within our body. Unity and peace are within us, and we will know the hunger and the happiness of all the lives within us. We *can* reach that state where all lives exist together in one place.

If you read the life history of 'Umar 'ibnul-Khattāb, may Allah be pleased with him, and if you read of his justice and his judgments, you will find it was very exalted. It was the kind of judgment that man and even God can praise. That is how he ruled the kingdom in his time. If any of us can reach that state of justice and perform that judgment, then we will be in the state of Islam or spotless purity. Anyone who does not have this state of justice is not in Islam. If we had this state of justice, we would see no separation. We would not find fault in anyone. We would not find differences in anyone. We would not harm any life. We would not kill any life. We would never sin. We would treat all lives as our own life. We would judge ourselves first, and then, if someone asked for help, we would give him justice. As soon as we thought of hurting someone, we would pass judgment against ourselves.

If we can have this state of justice and judgment and if we can perform this within ourselves, that is what we call the station of *īmān* and Islam. That is the station of the true believer [*mu'min*]. Those who do not have this sense of justice are the people who murder and kill and commit sins. They attack and hurt others. They laugh at the difficulties of others. They laugh at others being murdered. They take pride in others being murdered. They see torture as a pleasure. Such a person is not in a state of Islam.

If a person recognizes the difficulties of others as his own difficulties, that is Islam. One who has that awareness becomes Islam. To see the suffering of others as one's own suffering and to see the happiness of others as one's own happiness is Islam. To see the hunger of others as his own hunger is Islam. To see the life of others as his own life is Islam. To see the sweetness in the life of others and the happiness in the life of others as his own happiness is Islam.

If we could understand this sense of justice, there would not be any difficulties or murder in all three worlds (the world of the soul, this world, or the next world). Every second we would say, "*Al-hamdu lillāh*. All praise is to God!" And we would have *shukūr*, or contentment. Once this understanding comes within us and once we practice this perfect justice within ourselves, then we become true believers. We become the messengers of God, we become the lights of God, and we become the leaders of the kingdom of God. We must reflect on this, my very precious children.

Each one of us must pass judgment upon ourselves. Judging from within our own heart, we must realize our own faults. We must realize that we are the ones who have committed so many faults. We must realize that our eyes have committed many faults, our nose has committed many faults, our ears have committed many faults, our tongue has spoken so many faults, and the desires of our body are faults. We have to realize the faults of our hands and legs, such as when our legs kicked others. Realizing all this, we must pass judgment for our own faults.

Before we try to destroy someone else, we

should first pass judgment on ourselves. Before finding fault with others, we must first pass judgment upon ourselves. Before we backbite others, we must first pass judgment upon ourselves. Before we lie about others, we must first judge ourselves. Before we hurt the heart of another, we must first pass judgment on ourselves. Like that, we have to pass judgment on our thoughts and on all actions done by our eyes, ears, nose, hands, and mouth. The guilty ones are within our own body and mind. These are our qualities which exist in our actions. All these qualities exist within us, do they not? So we have to pass judgment on them. That is the state of *Īmān-Islām*. That is what is called Islam.

To first see the fault in yourself and then to pass judgment and correct yourself is true justice. Those who perform that justice are in the religion of truth. They are the leaders of the religion of truth. They are in the state of *Īmān-Islām*. They are the true believers.

If we fail to judge ourselves and instead attack others, then our actions will not be acceptable within the true sense of justice. Neither God nor man will accept such behavior. We must think about this. If we think about this and act accordingly, if we perform judgment and justice correctly, and if we stop attacking other lives, that will bring splendor to our lives.

We need a pure place in which to worship, is it not so? If we do not have such a place, how can we worship God? The one who worships God must be pure; his heart must be pure. If our hearts are pure, we can worship God in the state of purity. If we have no sense of justice in us, how can we pray to Him? These are the qualities one needs for prayer and worship. We must try to realize and understand this.

My very precious children, my jeweled lights, you must try to establish this state. My loving children, each one of us must try to reduce the weights and loads we carry with us. We must get rid of our burdens; we must try. The way we conduct ourselves now is the cause of all this trouble.

All my children, we must think about our own lives. We must think about the duty and actions of God. We must try to understand them and try to live in that state. Let our prayer be in that state, and let us try to reach the throne of God. That will be the splendor in our lives. That is the exaltedness of man and the clarity of our wisdom.

That is the advancement of our soul and the wealth of the three worlds. May we reach that. Amen. Amen.

My very precious children, my jeweled lights, may each one of you please think about this. Try to walk along the right path, and let us try to judge ourselves. To worship God is easy, but to understand the qualities and to go along this path is difficult. So let us strive to reach that station. Amen. Amen.

*As-salāmu 'alaikum wa Rahmatullāhi wa Barakātuhu Kullāhu.* May the peace of God and His beneficence be upon all of you. Amen.

# The Light
of the Prophets

*Bismillahir-Rahmanir-Rahim:* In the name of God, the Most Gracious, the Most Merciful. That God of undiminishing love and limitless grace, that God who gives us that undiminishing wealth of grace, may all responsibility and trust be to that God alone. Amen.

My precious jeweled lights, the beings who are the life within my life, my loving children who are born with me and who are the happiness of my heart, may God protect, sustain, and nourish each and every one of us. Amen. May God bestow His wonders and His benevolence upon us. May He give us His kingdom of grace and protect us. Amen. In this world and in the next world, in the world of the souls and in the realm of divine knowledge, may He protect, sustain, and nourish us. Amen.

May all our words, our intentions, our actions, our conduct, and our service be on the path of God, and may He give us His grace. Now and forever, in wealth and in poverty, in life and in death, may He guide us along the straight path. May He help us, may He hold onto us, may He beautify our hearts, may He make our wisdom light, and may He give us comfort. Amen. Amen.

All praises and praisings are to You alone. May You protect and sustain all lives. You are the only One worthy of prayer, You are the only One who can judge, and You are the only One who can dispense justice. You remain as that only One. You are the One who accepts, who listens, who inquires, and who judges. It is only You, O Allah. May You protect, sustain, and nourish us. Amen.

O God of all these names, the One who has limitless actions, the One who is the clarity of all these intentions, the One who is the grace and who gives meaning to everything, the One who is beyond the beginning and the end, the One who understands our intentions and dreams, the One who protects during sleep and during wakefulness, the One who is intermingled in happiness and in sorrow, the One who has no example, O Allah, *Ill Allāhu*, how can I ever describe Your resonance, Your meaning, Your effulgence, Your light, and the effulgence of Your completeness. O Almighty One who understands everything, at all moments, may You protect, sustain, and nourish us. Amen. Amen.

O the One of limitless grace, the One who is in want of nothing, O that One who gives joy to all lives, may You come and embrace us. May You feed us with Your grace and with Your wisdom. We need Your love. May Your love always be with us. Amen.

My precious jeweled lights, my brethren who are born as life within my life, are we not all of one family? Are we not brothers and sisters? All who are older than us are our older sisters and brothers, or our fathers and mothers. All who are younger than us are our younger brothers and sisters. This is the way we were related when we came to this world. Just as the rays were intermingled in the world of the souls, so they are intermingled in this world also. Just as we were intermingled then, should we not be forever joined together?

My precious jeweled lights, the light that was in the world of the souls is the same light that has come to this world. That grace which was there is the grace which is here. That plenitude which was there is here. That wisdom of light which was there is here. It is that same grace of that *Rahmatul-'ālamīn* [the Mercy and Compassion of all the universes] then, now, and forever. My precious jeweled lights, let us think of this. My children born with me as my brothers and sisters, what is it that we are sharing here, and what did we bring from there? We must understand this.

The section that we have taken from this earth and that we have accumulated here is of earth, fire, water, air, and ether. Within this we have accumulated mind and desire, and within that we have four hundred trillion, ten thousand illusions. The energies of air and the energies of all illusions are used for tricks. It is these *saktis* or forces that we have taken in.

There are two aspects of form: the body made of cells and the many various energies or *saktis*. Together these two have taken many hundreds of millions of forms. These forms are created out of earth, they eat from the earth, and they grow from the earth. They are praised on the earth, they are blamed on the earth, and finally they fall back to the earth again. This is the creation of the world. Everything that has this bodily form is like this. The shrubs, the grass, the herbs, the birds, the donkeys and horses, whatever we see, everything is like this. This is the state of creation.

Now, a tree bears a fruit, and when it is overripe it falls to the earth. But if the farmer nurses the tree carefully and if he plucks the fruit at the right time, then it can appease someone's hunger and give them comfort. It will give them solace and comfort their body. That is the usefulness of the fruit. But if it passes that stage and becomes overripe, it just drops to the earth and begins to spoil. Then it starts decomposing; it splits apart and oozes with fluid. The fruit disappears. Some of its seeds are destroyed, and some of the seeds grow again.

Similarly, this body is born from the earth. It grows from the earth, and like the grass, shrubs and trees, it finally perishes in the earth. See, my precious jeweled children, how the leaves of the trees fall to the earth. See how beautiful the shrubs and the grass are for a short time. But as soon as there is a snowfall, they all fade away. See how the leaves are dropping now. All of creation is in this state. We cannot depend on creation.

My precious jeweled lights, if we reflect on this, we will realize that at every moment, we must see what is needed and give whatever help we can. We must give comfort to other lives. We must do our duty and help others, just as the tree does its duty. If we miss that chance, then we will fall just like the apples fall. And if we fall, we only hurt ourselves and we will suffer. It will hurt our minds, and our lives will have no peace. A limitless number of diseases will overtake us, and our lives will finally disappear into the same thing that we came from. And just as the apple seed grows again, we will return to this world again.

Now see how the man plants the first apple tree. See how nicely he plows the earth, fertilizes, and plants the seed with great care. But after the apple falls, its seeds grow without cultivation. It falls on the earth which has not been plowed or fertilized, and even though the conditions are not optimal for its growth, it grows again. If the apple misses its chance and falls, this is how it is. There will be no help from the farmer who tended it before. It just falls off and decays. It missed its chance, and its seed has been planted in soil that has not been plowed. After a while, that seed will also disappear; it will not grow properly. Even if it does grow, that tree will not bear fruit. And even if it does bear fruits, they will be ridden with worms. Or else that seedling will die because another tree is growing too close, or perhaps because it cannot take deep root. At any rate, the tree will be diminished in its stature.

Similarly, my precious jeweled lights, God has made this life very carefully and sent us here. We have to reach maturity in this life. And within the time we have, if we do not do our duty, if we do not search for what we need to search for, if we do not reach that place which we have to reach, if we do not take what we have to take, then we will miss our chance and we will fall. Then if we take another birth, we will grow in a state of diminished wisdom, like the apple seed that grows on soil which has not been cultivated.

It is like that, my precious jeweled lights. Let us think of our births. All that we take from this earth will finally disappear; we will leave it behind. All that we eat will finally go back to the earth. Whatever we search for will be consumed by this one-span stomach, and all that is consumed by the one-span stomach will be discarded by the one-span stomach. That is what happens.

We will leave behind all that we have accumulated, and we will go back as we came.

My precious jeweled lights, let us think of each and every thing. We must try to find out what is this state of maturity we have to achieve. Let us think and analyze this, section by section. Let each of us reflect on this. We must understand, "What is it that came? And what is it that disappears?"

There were 124,000 prophets who came. They all came, and they all spoke. They all received the revelations and grace of God, and they have all gone back. Where have they gone? Where did God come from? Where has He gone? We must think of this. Have the prophets who came gone away? Have they all died? Have they remained here, or have they disappeared? We must think about this.

We saw each of the prophets as a body like ours made of earth, fire, water, air, and ether. Isn't that what we saw? It was the same body that we are carrying today. But they left this body and went on. What we saw, they left behind. We must think, "What is it that we need to understand?" Has Allah gone away? Have the *rasūls*, the messengers, gone away? Will we go away, or are we always here? Who are the *rasūls*? Who is Allah? If we had really seen the *rasūls*, would those *rasūls* have died? No, they would never have died. If we understood God, would He have gone? No. If we understood ourselves, would we ever die? No, we would never die.

Everything in totality, all the 18,000 universes, are within the heart of a true human being. The heart of a true man is the throne of God known as the *'arshul-mu'min*. It is heaven, and it is also hell. Heaven, hell, the prophets, and God all exist there. There is the *dhāt* and the *sifāt* [the essence and the manifestation], the *sirr* and the *sifāt* [the secret and the manifestation], and the *khair* and the *sharr* [right and wrong]. All exist within the heart of man.

So what is it we saw and what is it that has left? What we saw of the prophets was the form. That form or *surāt* belongs to the world. What is it that came and will remain? That is the light of God. His benevolence is here and never leaves. The body will leave, and all we see in the creation will leave. But if we could see that light, we would know that it never leaves.

If we tap on a rock, there will be a spark. Within whatever we tap there will be fire, and within whatever we melt there will be water. Whatever we split open will have air inside, and whatever we analyze will have the section of earth. Whatever we look at has illusions. And within everything, there is the soul. Within every soul, there is a light. It is there, is it not? Has it gone?

What we saw is wrong. What we understood as ourselves is wrong. What we understood as the prophets is also wrong. And the way we understood God is also wrong. We thought of Allah as if He had a form, but Allah is a light, an effulgence. And what did we see of the prophets? We saw only their forms. But the real prophet is a light, the light of *īmān* or absolute faith which comes from God and resides within the innermost heart, the *qalb*. The light of *īmān* ensures that the waves of the heart do not well up and cause the heart to tremble. It is this light which came.

Wisdom, light, completeness, compassion, love, and the words of God reside within the heart. They exist within everything. It is only the body that comes and goes. What we brought from there really does exist here. It is here. So what disappeared? The prophets? They did not disappear. Does an apple tree disappear? If an apple tree dies, its seeds remain and plant after plant keeps growing. The apple tree leaves but its seeds continue to germinate and grow, generation after generation. That potentiality is within, so we cannot say the apple tree has disappeared. Individual apple trees will come and go, but that tree which is in the seed will never die; it continues to reproduce.

Like that, nothing that came from God's essence ever dies. It is what we accumulate here which will go back to the earth. What came from the earth will go back to the earth; what we see will leave. And so it is with our body. But the true treasure never leaves. Only the material things go: the earth, fire, water, air, ether, and illusion or *māya* that we have accumulated will all leave. But the light of truth which is Allah is always within us and never leaves. Allah is the One who gives peace to all lives and makes all lives move and grow. That light is within all lives. That treasure is indeed here. It has not gone.

Where should we look for that light? We can search for that light within ourselves. How can we search for the prophets? If we look within, we will realize what that light is, and we will discard the body. We will search for wisdom, for divine knowledge, and for that light. Then we will know the prophets. We will discard our view of the prophets as forms, and we will see them as lights. Then we will see their treasure. But instead of doing this, we have embraced the body and made it into statues of gold, earth, stone, and wood. This is what we have kept. If we had not accepted this, we would have seen the light. If we had discarded these things, we would have seen the form of God.

If we could discard our form, then we would see that light form. If we could discard all the things that were given as examples of God, then we would know that light. If we could discard all that we have seen, all that we have accumulated, and all that we have experienced, then we could see that light.

We must understand that this treasure never left. It is only what we saw that has gone. We saw the body, and that body has gone away. We saw the form, and that form has gone. That belongs to the world. There is an estimate or a limited time for that. We must see that inestimable product within ourselves and within Him. That is the *alif, lām*, and *mīm*; these three are all in one place. The *mīm* is Muhammad, may God's peace and blessings be upon him, the *lām* is the *Nūr,* the resplendence of God, and the *alif* is Allah, exalted is His glory. These three exist in one and the same place. There is no place where these three do not exist.

We must cut off and discard all that we have seen and accumulated. Whatever form we see must be thrown away. That belongs to the creation. That is the *sifāt* [the manifestation of creation]. There are two sections: the *dhāt* or the essence, and the *sifāt*, or the manifestation. The *sifāt* is creation, and you must discard it. How must we see the prophets? Not in the manifested form, but in the form within that form, the light form, the essence.

*Qul: Huwallāhu ahad*—Say: He is God, the
    One and Only

*Allāhus-samad*—God, the Eternal, Absolute

*Lam yalid wa lam yūlad*—He begetteth not,
    nor is He begotten

*Wa lam yakul-lahu kufuwan ahad*—And
    there is none like unto Him.

He is the *Ahad*, the Only One. Allah, exalted is His glory, is within each and every thing, existing as the Absolute One. *Allāhus-samad:* He is the One who exists equally in all lives. *Lam yalid:* He exists on the right side as well as the left side. He alone shows His compassion in this world as well as in the hereafter. He is the One who exists equally for the poor and the rich. *Wa lam yūlad:* He always exists on the right side. *Wa lam yakul-lahu:* His entire life is on the right side. His kingdom is governed on the right side. *Kufuwan ahad:* He is the Absolute One within everyone and everything. He is the *Ahad.*

If we can understand that treasure, then we will realize that all the forms we can see are manifestations and that God can be understood as the essence within these forms. That is the secret within creation.

My precious jeweled lights, if we have seen the prophets as a form, a body, then they have left us, they have gone, and they have died. But if we have seen the light within their bodies, then the prophets will exist forever and will never leave us.

Without that ray from God, we could not be alive. If we could see the light of God, we would know that it would never leave us. But if we see ourselves as the body, then at some time that body will have to leave. It has an estimate. It has an alloted time. Whatever we see and accumulate will all leave; everything will go. But if we can understand and keep the light, the prophets, and Allah within us, then they will never leave; they are always with us.

To understand what is within us, we need a teacher, or Sheikh. What kind of Sheikh do we need? And what is it that we have to understand? Look at the difference between the way a chicken, a fox, and a dog search for food. What will the fox do? It will howl and run in search of another life to kill. If a dog needs food, it will run to find a bone. It will search for a bone, for something that smells, or for some feces. But if a chicken needs food, it will scratch the earth. It does not run in search of food; its habit is to scratch the earth where it is. Whatever else may be there—gold or silver or gems—the chicken will take only the worms and insects for its food. The chicken doesn't run around like the dog or the fox. Its job is to stay where it is and scratch the earth. It doesn't run after another life to appease its hunger like the dog or the fox, nor does it hunt like a lion. These other animals only have peace if they kill another life and eat it. They must roam and search for their food.

The Sheikh is like this chicken. He will scratch where he is, and from there he will take his food. He will go on scratching within himself, and he will discard all that the world brings. Whether it be gold or gems, he will throw all those things away. If the chicken can throw them away, why can't the wisdom of a true man do the same? Should a man take what the chicken has discarded? Even the chicken doesn't find any value in such things. Should the wisdom of a true man find any value in such things? They have no value for wisdom. They are of no value to that essence of God. A Sheikh will go on scratching and then discard all that.

The difference between a chicken and a Sheikh is that the chicken is scratching for worms to eat, but the Sheikh is scratching for God's light and His benevolence. He will discard the values and the titles of the world and take in the grace of God's light and the benevolence of God. This is what he will receive and take within. He throws away the worms and insects of the world, the gold and titles of the world, and takes the grace and the light of God. He will go on scratching and digging within himself.

When a Sheikh teaches you, he will ask you

to scratch within yourself. He will tell you, "Scratch within, scratch within."

You might get a little angry. "What is this? He is asking me to throw away my food. He is asking me to throw away my titles, my learning, my gems, my gold. He must be a fool who is trying to kill me. I keep on scratching, but I don't see anything here!"

Only if you discard these things will you receive what you are scratching for. Now when you scratch on one side, you will look at your title and say, "This fool is telling me to get rid of this. I have my title on this side." When you scratch on the other side, you will say, "My food is here, but he says to throw it away. What is this fool telling me?" The mind thinks like this on both sides. But to get to God, you must push all these things aside. Only then will you be able to reach His light and grace.

You have accumulated these worms, titles, gold, silver, and wealth. When the prophets tell you to dig these things up and discard them, it is difficult for you to do so. This is the message that the prophets brought. But what did we see? We only saw the forms of the prophets. That is why we have difficulty. Had we seen the light that they brought, things would not be difficult. The light of the prophets has not gone; it is here. We can see and speak to each and every prophet.

Wherever you look, God is there. But is He a rock or a stone or a sun or a moon or a bone? No. His sound is there, and His warnings are there. You can see Him. You can see His sound, His words, His speech. You can listen to the commandments given to the prophets, because they have not gone away. They are within us.

What could be seen has gone, and what we took in has gone. With these things, we cannot see that true treasure. What we saw has gone. But if we want to see what we should see, it is here. It has not gone. Since the very beginning, all of creation has been like this. All creations have the *sirr* and the *sifāt*, the mystery and the body, the *Dhāt* and *sifāt*, the essence and the manifestation. The *Dhāt* exists forever, but since the beginning of time the *sifāt* has had to leave. What came from the earth disappears, but what came from God always exists. The hereafter and heaven is within us. Birth and hell are within us. All are within us. The state of falsehood and truth are within us. Praise and blame are within us.

My precious jeweled lights, each one of my children, I have to scratch the way the chicken scratched. I have to show you the meaning of *īmān* and *Islām*, *khair* and *sharr*. Until we discard what we have kept within us, until we discard what we love and hold onto, the Sheikh has to go on scratching and showing us. If we do not do this, how can we become a true human being? If we are like the fox or the dog, or if we are like a tiger or a lion, then we have to kill other lives to eat. This is the world. These are the qualities of the animals. But if we are true human beings, then we must discard these qualities and say, "Go away! Go to the other side." We must understand what it is that we need.

We have to relish the light of God and the benevolence of God. His grace and His life or *hayāt* should be our food. It is this benevolence that we must absorb. Until that time we have to go on scratching.

This is what a true Sheikh will do. Maybe it will hurt you. Maybe it will be difficult for you. You have to think. You must understand that he is trying to make you scratch and search within yourself. He will say, "See what is within you. You are not as you are seeing yourself. Discard this and look within yourself. Scratch what is within that." This is what the Sheikh will tell you. That is his job.

If we reach that state, then there is no leaving and returning, there is no birth and death. Then we will die before death. Everything else within us will have left and only Allah will remain. We will have discarded everything, and we will remain here forever. Then everything else will have died, and we will never die. Let us think about this.

My precious jeweled lights, we must think of every seed. All that God has sent exists here. None of the prophets left, my children. What came from the earth is in the earth, but what they brought is here forever. You need to search for that. If you dig in the earth you will find earth, but if you dig even deeper, you will see that the prophets are still here. They are here. Dig within yourself and see your Father. You will find Him there. To do that, you need wisdom, you need $\bar{im\bar{a}n}$ and you need truth. There is one point only, and that is the peace and peacefulness. To have the qualities of God, we have to throw away everything that we call 'mine,' and then we will see the light from within.

You have to search. But do you need to go to the jungle? Do you need to go to a cave? Do you need to go here or there? No, you need not go anywhere. What you have to find is wisdom. What you have to search for is *īmān* and God's qualities. For that, you need an *Insān Kāmil Sheikh*, a realized teacher. Through his direction you must change. With his help you must go on digging and scratching. This is what is necessary.

My precious jeweled lights, it is getting late and we have to stop now. If we are alive tomorrow, we will talk some more.

Each one of my children should think. There is no point in our having seen the bodies of the prophets and carrying that with us. All that came from the earth has disappeared in the earth. The bodies of the prophets, your body, the trees, the shrubs, the fruits, everything is like that. But if you could see that which grew from God, you would know that it has never left. It exists here. Think of this. It has remained here, and if you look within yourself, you will see it.

My precious children, if you understand each

point in this manner, then you can really understand. Let us think of this. *Āmīn, Ya Rabbil-'ālamīn, Al-hamdu lillāh:* So be it, O Ruler of the universes. All praise be to God.

the length and breadth of the seven oceans of desires [*nafs*]; that which awakens all the truths which have been destroyed and buried in the ocean of illusion [*māya*]; that which awakens true *īmān;* that which explains the state of purity to each life [*hayāt*] in the same way that it existed in the beginning of creation [*awwal*]. The grace of the essence of God [*Dhāt*], which gives the life [*hayāt*] of purity back and which makes it into the divine vibration.

It is also a name which has been given to Allah. He can be addressed as *Yā Qutb* or *Yā Quddūs* [the Holy One]. *Quddūs* is His *wilāyat* [power or miracle], while *Qutb* is His action. *Wilāyat* is the power of that action.

Lit.: axis, axle, pole, pivot. A title used for the great holy men of Islam.

*qutbiyyat* (A)  The wisdom of the *Qutb;* the sixth state of consciousness; divine wisdom; divine analytic wisdom; the wisdom which explains the truth of God. The wisdom that is the power [*wilāyat*] of the *Qutb*. That which awakens all the truths which have been buried, lay hidden, or destroyed in the ocean of illusion [*māya*]. That which awakens true *īmān*.

*rahmat* (A)  God's grace; His forgiveness and compassion; His benevolence; His wealth. To all creations, He is the wealth of life [*hayāt*] and the wealth of *īmān* [absolute faith, certitude, and determination]. All the good things that we receive from God are His *rahmat*, the wealth of God's plenitude. If man can receive this, that is very good.

Everything that is within God is *rahmat*, and if He were to give that grace, it would be an undiminishing, limitless wealth. That which has been discarded from Him is the world's wealth and treasures. Those treasures can perish and be destroyed and are subject to change. The word *rahmat* can also be used for those worldly treasures that change with the seasons. But the *rahmat* of Allah will never change for all time. That is why it is the greatest, most valuable treasure to anyone who receives it.

*Rahmatul-'ālamīn* (A) The Mercy and Compassion of all the universes. The One who gives everything to all His creations. He makes them arise by saying, "*Kun!* Be!" and then He gives whatever they need, and He comforts and rules over them.

*rasūl* (A) Apostle or messenger. One who has wisdom, faith in God, and good qualities. One who behaves with respect and dignity toward his fellow man. A *rasūl* is one who has accepted only God and has rejected everything else, one who has accepted God's divine words, His qualities and actions and puts them into practice. Those who from time immemorial have been giving the divine laws of God to the people. Those who have such a connection with God have been called a prophet [*nabī*] or *rasūl*. The name *rasūl* has been given even to the angels.

*Yā Rasūl* is a name given to Prophet Muhammad (*Sal.*).

*rishi* (T)   An inspired sage. *Rishis, muktars, munivars,* and *siddhars* are all the same—they perform magic and miracles. They derive their inspiration from the energy of the mind and from the five elements (earth, fire, water, air, and ether). Inspirations received from the energies [*saktis*] of the five elements emerge from their hearts and are revealed outside. These inspirations do not come from God; they come from the elements and the 64 arts [*kalai*].

*sakti* (T)   A force or energy. In Tamil, the word *sakti* refers to *Shiva-Sakti*. *Sakti* is the consort of *Shiva* [both are deities in Hinduism]. In Arabic, *Shiva* and *Sakti* are called *Ādam* and *Hawwā'*, and in Christianity they are Adam and Eve. They are the original father and mother, but they are given various names and meanings in the different religions and languages.

(*Sal.*) (A)   Abbreviation for *Sallallāhu 'alaihi wa sallam*.

*Sallallāhu 'alaihi wa sallam* (A)   God bless him and grant him salvation. A supplication traditionally spoken after mentioning the name of Prophet

Muhammad *(Sal.)*. Saying, *"Sall-allāhu 'alaihi wa sallam,"* therefore means: "In the same way that you gave peace to us, may all the people who follow the Prophet be blessed with eternal and undiminishing peace."

*sharr* (A)   That which is wrong, bad, or evil, as opposed to *khair* [right].

*shukūr* (A)   Contentment; the state within inner patience [*sabūr*]; that which is kept within the treasure chest of patience. *Yā Shakūr*—one of the 99 beautiful names of Allah. To have *shukūr* with the help of the One who is *Yā Shakūr*, is true *shukūr*.

*siddhar* (T)   One who performs magic and tricks [*siddhis*] or who has supernatural abilities obtained by devotion to and control of the elements. One who performs magic using a five-lettered mantra [*panchan charum*] relating to the five elements of earth, fire, water, air, and ether.

One who prays to and controls the energies of the earth, the mind, illusion, demons and spirits. He depicts these energies as gods or goddesses, recites mantras, and worships them. Through the mantras certain gases are formed within the body. Those gases are materialized and manifested outside as the energies [*saktis*] which he utilizes to perform various occult powers [*siddhis*] in the world. He may walk on water or fire, he may pick

# The World Within and Without

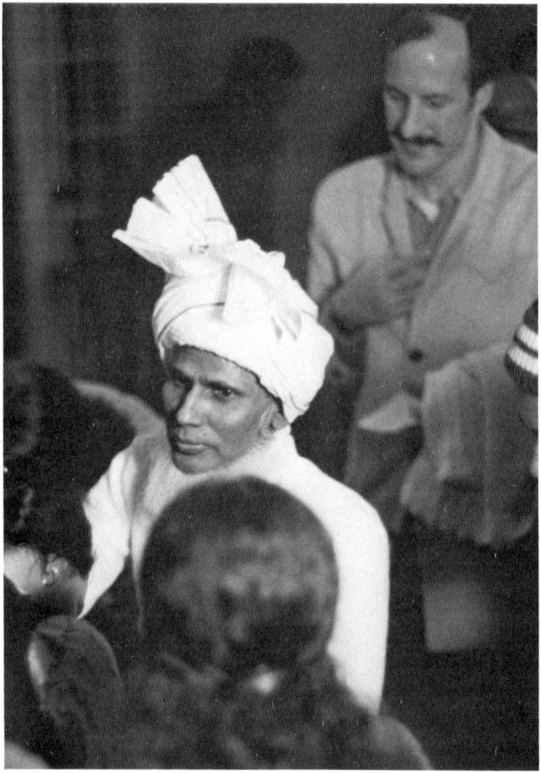

*Bismillāhir-Rahmānir-Rahīm:* In the name of God, the Most Merciful, the Most Gracious.

May Allah, the unfathomable ruler of grace, the One who is incomparable love and gives undiminishing wealth, the One who gives the fragrance which the mind cannot perceive, grant you His resonance, His explanation, the radiance of wisdom, and the plenitude of the clarity of the soul. May He give and give this to you, protect you, and nourish you.

Children, may the treasure of the heart known as *Allāhu* which gives and gives but never diminishes, protect you and give you grace. Children, may He protect you, all your brothers and sisters, all your relations, all your friends, all who are with you, all the devotees of God, all who have wisdom, and all who are intermingled with your love. May God protect all of you. May the wealth of grace which is known as *Allāhu* fill your hearts, overflow from your hearts, and resonate and shine from your hearts as the light of the grace of wisdom. Amen.

May all of you dispel the disease known as the world, the dog known as desire, the demon known as the mind, the torpor known as illusion, the pleasure that is the dream, the sadness that is the darkness of ignorance, the karma that is the torpor of the world, the evil actions of *kalam* [time, which is comprised of arrogance, karma, and illusion] that lead you to *Kalan* [the Angel of Death], and the nature and games of the five elements that collect and praise time. May you dispel all these things and go beyond them to Allah, the original treasure which stands in the open space, the treasure of the innermost heart. May God give you the grace of His wisdom to dispel all these evils. Amen. May God fill your hearts with His grace. Amen.

Children, may you be given exalted wisdom, exalted conduct, exalted patience, exalted truth, the exaltedness of God's compassion, and the exaltedness of good thoughts and good intentions. May God give you more and more of this grace. Precious jeweled lights of my eyes, may God give all of you long lives without illness, undiminishing wealth, the clear treasure of wisdom which will not be hypnotized by the mind, the wealth of the might of grace, and the determination and certitude of faith in God which is untouched by the evil actions and torpor of the elements. I am praying that God give you this grace. Amen.

Precious jeweled lights of my eyes, we have been born as human beings. In this world, man has been called the most wondrously clear and wise creation. It has been said that the existence of man is very rare and unique. Man is a mystery to the world, and the One who created the mystery known as man is also a mystery. Man-God, *Insān Kāmil,* or perfected man is the mystery within the mystery. That is the mysterious power of Allah.

God is the mystery which resplends in perfection [*kamāl*], and *Insān Kāmil* is the mystery within the mystery. When the two become one, existing as wisdom within wisdom, as speech within speech, as prayer within prayer, as meditation within meditation, as sound within sound, as food within food, and as life within life—that is the mystery. When the two intermingle and dwell as one within one, that is the secret. That is the secret within the secret. That mystery exists when God is within man and man is within God.

Man is a mystery to God, and God is a mystery to man. Resonating as a resonance, explaining and shining as an explanation, radiating as a radiance, this state and this secret will be known by man. God will be known by man, man will be known by God, and man and God will dwell in one place. In that state, man is a secret within God, and God is a secret within man. Precious children, jeweled lights of my eyes, in this state man is truly a man. This is what man must realize in this world; he must realize the rarity of his birth.

Precious children of this funny family, this tiny ant man has an explanation as small as he is:

    Pretend to believe in the world
    But do not believe in it.

The meaning: Not everyone born with the form of man is a man, and not everything that lives in the world has wisdom. Of all the things that appear in the world, there is not one that does not kill, and there is not one that does not eat. Nothing that lives in the world lives without hunger, illness, old age, or death. Everything that has a form made of the five elements has hunger, illness, old age, and death.

It is said that when hunger comes, the ten good qualities and the divine analytic wisdom which distinguishes and sees, fly away. The pangs of hunger can destroy wisdom. The selfishness of the body exists as desire, blood-ties, attachments, religions, races, castes, separations, philosophies, scriptures, differences, praise, and blame.

There are 17 *purānas,* or ancient epics, which make up the world—arrogance, karma, and *māya,* or illusion; the three sons of *māya: tārahan, singhan,* and *sūran;* lust, hatred, miserliness, greed, fanaticism, envy, intoxicants, desire, theft, murder, and falsehood.

Creation is the world in which you now exist and in which you are now studying. The qualities of all the 17 *purānas* exist in the creations of this world. The creations catch and eat each other, kill each other, conquer each other, hypnotize each other, drink each other's blood, praise each other, and blame each other. They perform four hundred trillion, ten thousand kinds of spiritual miracles, energies, mesmerism, magics, mantric magic, illusory magic, sexual games, arts, sciences, and sexual teachings.

The beauty of form, the visions seen by the eyes, the music heard by the ears, the smells smelled by the nose, the tastes tasted by the tongue, all the energies of the five elements, the qualities of the 17 *purānas*, and the millions and millions of shadows within the *purānas* are all contained in the huge world that exists within the heart of man. That world contains the 18,000 universes. It lies within man, and man lies within it.

Sometimes man praises the world and sometimes he blames it. Sometimes it makes him happy and sometimes it makes him sad. Man thinks that he can reach liberation in this world, and he studies its histories. Because he exists in that state, he might try to catch, kill, and eat, praise or blame any of the creations. But actually, man contains the world within himself.

Children, the intellect of man can perceive that there are two worlds. One is within his heart, and the other is the world outside which is seen by his eyes and perceived by his senses. In this world of physical visions, he sees each creation and gives it a name, such as 'animal', 'dog', 'fox', 'tree', 'bush', 'vulture', 'eagle', or 'monkey'. These animals are visible to the eyes. When he looks at these works of art, he might write stories about them, sing songs about them, or praise them. But in both worlds, animals will come to try to kill a man of truth, a man of mystery. They will come to eat him and to destroy him. We must pretend to believe them. We must act in such a way as to deceive them, and then we must escape. Man must escape from these 'animals' in order to leave this world.

Man must understand this with mysterious wisdom. He must deceive those things, pretend to believe them, and then escape. If he believes in them, they will destroy and eat his unique birth. If he believes in them, they will kill his connection to that unique mystery. We must pretend to believe in them, deceive them, and escape. Otherwise, they will try to kill our connection to the Mystery, and they will try to kill us. This is one thing that the ant man says.

The second thought is:
> Believe in God
> Do not pretend to believe in Him.

Believe in God. Believe in the one point. Believe in the One God, the mysterious God. He will embrace and protect you. That one point is the mystery. Believe in the treasure which exists as man within God and God within man. Believe in that treasure. That will protect you. You can exist within it.

Do not pretend to believe in God. That will destroy you. If you pretend to believe in Him, that deception will destroy you. Believe in God with determination.

Children, precious jeweled lights within my eyes, this is what all who are with us and all who have taken the unique birth of man must know. We must try to know this state and act accordingly.

Children, the world exists in two ways. One way is outside. That is the world we can see. The birds, the reptiles, the four-legged animals, the eagles, the vultures, the thousand-legged insects, the eight-legged insects, the ten-legged insects, the six-legged beetles, the crawling worms, the elephants, the lions, the cats, the fish, the oceans, the lands, the mountains, the caves, the fire, the water, the air, the earth, the sky, the sun, the moon, the stars, the clouds, the flowers, the trees, the demons, the ghosts, the devils, the jinns, the fairies, the bears, the rhinoceroses, the countless and numberless million, million, billion, trillion creations, and all the things that have appeared can be seen on the outside.

From the tiny crawling ants and insects up to the largest of the creations, everything that appears has a *sakti*, or energy. Everything has certain abilities and miracles that they can perform. If an ant bites you, how you will squirm! That is its miracle. If a snake bites us, we will fall unconscious and possibly even die; that is its *sakti*. The birds fly in the sky and perform their *saktis* and miracles there. Eagles, vultures, and bats can see in places where human beings cannot, and they can find food through their sense of smell. They have those abilities. Tigers, bears, lions, and elephants all have the abilities and *saktis* to perform their miracles.

Showing their *saktis* and miracles, the trees, the fruits, and the flowers call out to entice the passersby, saying, "Come, come!" They call out to everyone. That is their *sakti* and their *siddhi*, or elemental miracle. The fruits and flowers all send out their fragrances and say, "Come, come. I am here." They fascinate everyone that goes by, and they show their miracles.

*Māya* shows its beauty, its sound, and its melody, and it pulls on man. Woman, possessions, land, and gold demonstrate their *saktis*, strengths, and miracles. They pull and hold onto man, trying to draw him to them and make him merge with them. Lust, hatred, and miserliness come to man and attack him. They say, "Hey! Come here, look at this! Look at that!" They catch him and bring him under their control. They say, "Don't get up. Stay. This is for you." Religions, castes, races, titles, and honors are also like that. Each one performs its own miracles and *saktis*. They are all miracles. Indeed, everything that can catch man has a miracle and a *sakti*.

There are many great and wondrous miracles in this world. There are four hundred trillion, ten thousand miracles and *saktis* that exist in the world. They try to catch man, control him, and make him worship them. They make him surrender and pay obeisance to them. Desires for gold, land, and women attack and attempt to catch and embrace man. They try to make him surrender to them and ask favors of them. Man *does* pray to such things. He meditates on them and asks them for wisdom and grace.

All these *saktis* must be looked at with wisdom. If we look at them with wisdom, we will see that they are diseases which can kill us. We will see that they are demons which can make us dance. We will see that they are the energies and miracles of ghosts, demons, ghouls, devils, and witches. Once a man is caught by these, he begins to make them his idols or gods, and he dedicates himself to them. He makes a snake his god. He surrenders to it and asks favors of it. The snake god gives him what it has, so he assumes the qualities and inner form of the snake. When man makes a lion his god and surrenders to it, the lion god gives him what it has—it gives him its qualities and form. When man makes an elephant his god, it gives him what it has—the triple dirt of arrogance, karma, and *māya*.

When man makes karma his god, everything connected to karma is given to him. When he makes a vulture his god, the vulture's qualities of eating corpses are given to him. When man makes an eagle his god, he takes on the qualities of a *siddhar*, one who flies and performs miracles in the sky, and the eagle's qualities of spotting and pouncing on rats, snakes, baby chicks, and cats.

When man makes a bull his idol and surrenders himself to it, he takes on the bull's form and the qualities of plowing the world, eating the world, and defecating on the world. He takes on the bull's qualities of jumping on another, without knowing whether it is his mother or child or another cow from the herd.

When he takes a horse for his god and surrenders to it, the form and qualities of the horse are passed on to him. When he makes a donkey his god, the form and qualities of the donkey are passed on to him. When he makes a pig his idol, the qualities of the pig are passed on to him. When he makes a rat his god, the qualities of treachery, deceit, and chewing holes become his qualities. When he makes a cat his god, he assumes the cat's qualities of stealing and drinking milk with its eyes shut. When he makes a fish his god, he receives the qualities of catching worms, swimming, and eating moss, insects, and filth.

When man makes water his god, all the worms, insects, beetles, dirt, and everything in the water are given to him. When he makes fire his god, the qualities of fire are given to him: the qualities of burning things and burning all the other gods, the qualities of anger, impatience, and temper. When he makes the earth his god, he is given the four hundred trillion, ten thousand colors and hues of the earth. When he makes the air his god, the vapors and spirits of all creation are given to him, along with mind, desire, attachments, and so many kinds of winds which can cause destruction—hurricanes, gales, thunderstorms, cyclones, and tornadoes. All the hurricanes and cyclones will be given to him. The qualities of the air will not allow him a second of peace.

This is how the four hundred trillion, ten thousand qualities of the spiritual forces and energies are given to man. All their differences are given to him. All the gods that are visible to him give him their qualities. And once they have given him their qualities, he dies within them. When he asks a favor of a lion, he becomes a lion. When he asks a favor of a donkey, he comes back in the form of a donkey. When he asks a favor of a dog, he comes back in the form of a dog. When he asks a favor of a monkey, he comes back in the form of a monkey. When he asks a favor of a demon, he comes back as a demon. When he asks a favor of a devil, he comes back to drink blood.

Like this, whatever he gives his attention to on the outside is what he will nourish on the inside. He takes everything which is outside and gathers it within himself. Outside they exist as forms, but inside, they exist as poisons, vapors, and spirits. The world of scenes, the scenes of acting in this elemental world, are all outside, and they are all gathered within the heart of man.

Therefore, my precious children, jeweled lights of my eyes, as we begin to realize and understand, everything we see on the outside as a form we will see within us as qualities and shadow forms which can subject us to many rebirths. The forms are outside, but all their energies, forces, miracles, and abilities appear in the heart of man.

The world he sees outside is a dot. The world inside is just an atom, but he places so many things inside the atom world, worshipping and surrendering to them. We must think of this state. And we must understand which of these two worlds we must come to know.

Man takes things with form, makes them

formless within himself, and then dies in that state. Then he takes that same form in his rebirth and loses his connection to God. He forsakes the name of Man-God and reappears in the form of a snake, a scorpion, a dog, a fox, a donkey, an elephant, a demon, a monkey, a poison, a crab, a bird, or a fowl. Whatever *sakti* he attains, whatever miracle he believes, whatever he trusts, whatever he surrenders to, and whatever qualities he takes into himself will be the form of his rebirth. In the end, he will be subject to one hundred and five million rebirths. He will be subject to all the four hundred trillion, ten thousand miracles and energies and will end up as a worm, an insect, and food for hell. This is the world man nourishes for himself.

Whatever *sakti* he prays to is the *sakti* and the form which will be created formlessly in his heart. Man will be reborn as whatever idol he prays to or places his intentions upon and whatever form he gives life to in his heart. As he gives his mind, his intellect, and his thoughts to those gods, as he makes love to those gods, a form is made and given life within him. That form, those qualities, those actions, those sounds, that behavior, that intelligence, and those abilities will come from the outside to the inside.

The same thing happens when a husband and wife join together. Their minds, their thoughts, and their love are made one when they make love. An embryo is formed in the energies they bring about. Their noises, their sounds, their beauty, and their voices are all stamped onto that embryo, and they come into form. The actions of the mother and the father come into the blood and tissues of the embryo. When the child is born, it will be similar to the mother or the father, in its appearance or in its sound, its qualities, or its actions.

When a man's mind, his intellect, and his devotion focus upon something, it is like the joining together of a man and a woman. The energies of the five elements (earth, fire, water, air, and ether) will exist within the form with which he joins, and there will be millions of differences within it. As he loves those qualities and intermingles with them every second and every day, those qualities, actions, behavior, and *saktis* will all come to exist within him. Just as the qualities of the parents come into a child, so these qualities will come into a man's heart.

In his devotion, man has to give those qualities whatever they require. He must feed whatever *sakti* he raises within himself and whatever *sakti* he makes use of. He must feed all those things according to their forms. Some must be given goats, some must be given chickens, some must be given murders, some must be given intoxicants, some must be given marijuana, some must be given beer, some must be given brandy, some must be given opium, some must be given LSD, some must be given other hallucinogenic drugs, some must be given women, some must be given blood. Whatever food is necessary for the *saktis* inside is the food they must be given. Man must form that food inside and give it to them. Each *sakti* that is formed in the heart, whether it be murder, sin, karma, or *māya*, must be given what it requires. Man must feed them if they are to grow.

That is the world within. If he raises the outside things inside and if he nourishes formed things formlessly, then he must become a slave and a servant to those things and must give them whatever they want. He must surrender to them and ask favors of them. He must take on their qualities, act with their actions, take repeated births, and eventually end up in hell. Then he will lose the connection to God and the connection to being a true man.

Whatever we raise, whatever we love, whatever we grow, whatever we serve, whatever we perform *pūjās* to and make offerings to, whatever we become a slave to, and whatever we make into a god will cause us to lose our connection to the true human being and our connection to God. We must all realize this with wisdom.

We must recognize these *saktis* within ourselves. We must not place our trust in them or surrender to their qualities. All the formless *saktis* of the inner world must be chased out. Without implanting any more *saktis* within us, we must chase out those already existing there. Those qualities, those elements, and those demons must be chased out and dispelled. All those forms must be dispelled.

Only when man loves the mystery within the mystery, the secret within the secret, the wisdom within wisdom, the life within life, and the resplendence within the resplendence which shines as man within man and which exists as the ray within the ray known as wisdom; only when he loves the nature of that mystery which exists as absolute purity, when he makes that mystery come to life within himself and surrenders to that mystery, only then does he become that mysterious treasure.

When he believes in that mystery and dedicates himself to that mystery; when he places its qualities, actions, and powers into the world of wisdom and the world of his soul within himself; when he makes that mystery come into form within himself and serves it; when he disappears as the mystery into the mystery; when he takes into himself God's 3,000 gracious and beautiful qualities, God's quality of seeing all other lives as His own and protecting all lives without giving way to hunger, old age, illness, or death; when he takes into himself goodness, the love of all lives, surrender, balance, concentration, patience, tolerance, peace, justice, honesty, and good conduct; when the qualities of God's mystery take form within him, and all God's actions exist within him, then the birth within him will be cut off. His destruction will have been destroyed.

Because God has no birth, a true man will have no birth. Because God has no darkness, he will have no darkness. God has no torpor, so he will have no torpor. God has no idols, so he will have no idols. God has no hunger, so he will have no hunger. God has no selfishness, so he will have no selfishness. God has no desire, so he will have no desire. God has no lust, so he will have no lust. God is not fascinated by women, so he will not be fascinated by women. God is not fascinated by owning land and by material things, so he will not be fascinated by these. God is not hypnotized by the mind, so he will not be hypnotized by the mind. God has no physical visions, so he will have no physical visions. God has no illness, old age, or death, so he will have no illness, old age or death. God's qualities do not change, so his qualities will not change. And because God is not fascinated by miracles, he will not be fascinated by miracles.

When God's incomparable and countless qualities and actions come to exist within man, man will exist in that mystery, he will have no birth or death, and he will have no evil. His state will be one of resplendent prayer to God, for prayer is to make God come into form within oneself. But if anything other than God is kept within—any animal to which man surrenders, any *sakti* he desires, any miracle he wants to perform, whether he would like to fly in the sky, rule the earth, or possess gold—then the qualities of these intentions will exist within him. In this state, the four hundred trillion, ten thousand miracles and qualities of the creations, their actions, and their forms will come into man. Taking on those actions, committing those murders, and committing those sins will subject him to many millions of rebirths. In the end, he will exist as a worm in hell.

Man considers this to be devotion; he considers this to be praiseworthy and miraculous. Because of this state, the creation with the face of man is subject to being ruled from within by animals. The qualities, the actions, the conduct, and the worship of animals come to exist within him. Finally, he dies with those animal actions. He dies in murder, sin, arrogance, and in the teachings of the 17 *purānas*. He dies and is reborn.

One who thinks with wisdom and takes God's form within himself will reach the state of Man-God, or *Insān Kāmil*. He will become one without form. He will become one who is forever mature. He will become one who is that mystery and is incomparable. He will become the plenitude which transcends beginning and end. He will become one who transcends separation, who has no birth or destruction, and who has no wife or child. He will become one who is not bound by the connection to *māya* and who has no desire, torpor or hunger.

It is the power of God that we must form within ourselves; to do this is prayer and worship. This must be formed within a true man or *Insān*. One who forms this power within himself will be without birth, death, diminishing or end. He will be the power within the power. He and God will be one; he and God will be in the same place; he and God will do the same work and have the same power.

Without this state, all the *saktis* man raises in his heart and all the scenes he sees in the outside world will take form within him, and they will become his idols. He will perform *pūjās* to them and take on their qualities, actions, and forms. This will result in many millions of rebirths.

One who does not take these *saktis* into himself will not be reborn. If he does not take these forms into himself, then he will have the form of man, the beauty of God, the qualities of God, the pure and resplendent light, and the beauty of the undiminishing and perfect treasure which transcends race and religion. He will be a king to the three worlds. He will be a messenger of God. He will be within God, and God will be within him. The two will be one and will rule the kingdom of God.

Only if this state comes within one can he truly be called a man. His form will be different, his actions will be different, his prayer will be different, and his power will be different. That power will be the connection between him and God. If we would all understand this and act accordingly, it would be good.

It is not the One who created man who has subjected him to these many rebirths, deaths, sadnesses, and happinesses. God gave all three worlds to man: the world of the soul, this earth world which is the world of hell, and the world of God which is the world of grace and wisdom. He gave man the potential to be the king of these three worlds. God gave the majesty of ruling these three world to man.

Two of these worlds exist within and one is seen on the outside. The world of hell is seen on the outside. That is the world of drama, the world of God's creation, the world of form, and the world of God's art. The 18,000 universes and everything in them, the seven layers of the earth and the seven realms of the sky, all the beauties and all the forms have been sculpted and revealed in this world of God's creation and artistry. The creations, the beings, their lives, their qualities, their food, their intellect, and their abilities have all been created so that we may understand our Father's artistry, and so that we may understand their qualities. We must study all the lessons our Father has given. We must praise our Father, accept His splendor, and know that He is more beautiful than any of those things. All the explanations and lessons in the creations in all the universes are His books. Each creation is one of God's books. They are all God's stories. Each reveals His secrets. Each reveals His mystery.

When we look at the beauty, the qualities, and the actions of the earth, the sky, the sun, the moon, the stars, the reptiles, the birds, the four-legged animals, the jewels, the water, the earth, the air, the fire, man, monkeys, ants, rats, and all creations, we can see that each of them contains one of God's stories. We must understand these stories and realize that there is no Father other than God, that He has no form, and that He has no shape. We must know this with determined faith.

We must act with the qualities of our Father. We must take form in those actions, becoming conceived within Him, becoming embryonic forms within Him, taking form within Him, becoming light within Him, receiving life within Him, receiving completion within Him, receiving the eye of wisdom within Him, receiving the nose of wisdom within Him, receiving the taste of the tongue of wisdom within Him, receiving the perception and the sounds of the ears of wisdom within Him, receiving His innermost heart within Him, receiving His undiminishing, unwanting, forever-giving hands of wisdom, receiving legs within Him which can walk through the whole world in one second, receiving the boon of never being hungry, and receiving eternal life without illness, old age, death, or birth. We must be conceived and take form within God's womb. We must grow within Him, and we must exist within Him forever.

When we are born from within God, we will be in the form of Man-God. When all those things are learned, when we establish ourselves in that state, the story born from within God will be Man-God, God-Man. The light body which is born from within Him is called His son. That form is the body of Man-God, the body of wisdom, the resplendent body. That resplendence dawns from within resplendence. It is formed within God and born from within Him. That is when the two bodies live as one body. That is when two aspects live in one place.

Jesus, peace be upon him, spoke of this. He said, "If man is not born again, he will not reach the kingdom of God." The meaning of this is that we must become an embryonic form within God, and we must know and understand the secrets and the stories of God in the three worlds. We must transcend this world and leave it behind, go to the world of God, be conceived within God, take form within God, receive grace within God, and receive His light, His qualities, His sound, His fragrance, His wisdom, His completeness, His purity, His beauty, and His taste.

When man dawns from within God and is born from within God, he will be the son of the kingdom of God. He will be God, and the two will rule the kingdom as One. This is the meaning of being born again. One must leave this world and go to that world, intermingle with God in that world, be conceived there, and be born from that embryonic state within Him. That is wisdom.

Children, precious jeweled lights within my eyes, wisdom exists in another world. There are two kinds of learning we must come to know. One is outside and one is inside. The world, religions, scriptures, books, philosophies, scenes, trees, flowers, bushes, jewels, and all outer things are one kind of learning. We see this outer world with our eyes, we hear its sounds in our ears, we smell the outer smells, we taste the outer tastes, we smile the outer smiles, and we speak the outer words. There is an outer aspect and an outer learning in all those things.

The things of the outer world can be studied through religions, through scriptures, through philosophies, through doctrines, through the *purānas*, through yogis, through *rishis* or sages, through animals, through the elements, through demons, ghosts, ghouls, and witches, and through illusory magic tricks which can extend to the skies. The outer world can be studied through many things like these. This outer world is the world of illusory energies called *māya sakti*, the world of demonic *saktis*, the world of elemental *saktis*. This outer world exists as one kind of learning. Those things can all be drawn in books and learned from books in so many millions of various languages, prayers, and miracles. These are the lessons we learn as outer meanings.

Whatever we like and pray to in this world will take form within us. It takes form, becomes an embryo, grows, and then we give birth to it. We give birth to it and raise it. These are the kinds of devotion that are subject to many millions of rebirths, to many millions of qualities, to many millions of kinds of actions, and to many millions of kinds of murders. These are the kinds of devotion that exist in many millions of ways. This is easy. Everyone can learn this.

But there is another kind of study. It is secret. It is the study of the kingdom of God, and it exists within. It transcends the seven innermost hearts and opens the eighth. The heart within that seventh heart will exist as the kingdom of God. It transcends the world of the elements, the world of fire, the world of earth, the world of desire, the world of water which is the world of creation, the world of air, and the world of the mind. It is the world of wisdom which is the world of God.

This learning is an entirely different section. This study is a mysterious secret. It does not exist in books, in scriptures, in religions, or in philosophies. It exists as God's grace, as His *qudrat* or power, as His benevolence, and as His mystery. It exists as God. It is the majesty of His kingdom, it is His perfection, and it is His justice.

That study cannot be found on the outside. Those who perform miracles do not have that learning. It is not within the doctrines of yogis, sages, and *rishis*. It is not within one who flies in the skies. It is not within one who walks on the water. Those things are merely arts known as *kalai gnānam*. That inner learning does not exist within one who can twist the earth into a rope. It is not within one who can make himself invisible to the eyes of others. It is not within one who can walk on fire. It is not within one who can tie up the mouth of a tiger. It is not within one who can make the world shake. None of those miracles exist in the section of inner knowledge. That study does not exist in people like this.

That study is called a mystery. One who is conceived in God and becomes an embryonic form in God and is born, transformed, from within God contains that mystery. One who is born in Him, one who grows in Him, one whose actions are within Him, and one who is intermingled with Him, contains that mystery. All the scenes of the world and all the elemental kingdoms will have been dispelled from within him. The kingdom of earth will have been dispelled from within him. The kingdom of fire will have been dispelled from within him. The kingdom of water will have been dispelled from within him. The kingdom of air will have been dispelled from within him. The kingdom of the spirits will have been dispelled from within him. The kingdom of desire will have been dispelled from within him. The kingdom of the mind will have been dispelled from within him. The kingdom of the elements will have been dispelled from within him. The kingdom of the demons will have been dispelled from within him. The kingdom of *māya* will have been dispelled from within him. And the kingdom of the sky will have been dispelled from within him.

One who goes beyond all these things and takes form within God will know the learning and the study of God's kingdom. He will be called a wise man, he will be called a messenger of God, and he will be called the son of God. He will dwell within God and God will dwell within him. One who is in this state, one who has that form, one who is born within God will be able to study that secret mystery. Only if one actually goes there can he see. Then he will be shown.

As one goes further and further, more and more exists to be known. As one puts one foot in front of the other, God's secrets will be revealed step by step. His wonders, His powers, His visions and His justice will be revealed. Man will come to know more and more as he goes further and further. That learning does not exist in writings; it is the mysterious study.

That study, children, is what is called wisdom. That is man; that is Man-God. The study of that kingdom belongs to one who is born again and transformed from his animal state. That study belongs to the child of God who comes to the state of Man-God. It belongs to one who takes form within God. This is a wondrous study.

Children, to study this is very difficult. This learning is a wonder and a mystery. God exists as a mystery, man exists as a mystery, and this learning exists as a mystery. This is the secret we must know. It is not easy. We must study in a very subtle manner in order to learn this. God must be conceived within us. He must become an embryonic form within us, and we must become an embryonic form within Him. God must come into form within man, and man must come into form within God. Man must be born within God, and God must be born within man. Only when that form comes can man reach God. First, God must be conceived within man. Then man must be conceived within God. Man must be born transformed and that interchange must take place. Man must merge with God and God must merge with him. To be born in this way is wisdom. That is the greatest wonder.

One who does not achieve this state will take on the qualities of monkeys, donkeys, lions, tigers, and elephants. He will form them within himself, surrender to them, and later he will be reborn as those animals. This is where those *saktis* lead to; this is where those *saktis* end.

Children, we must realize and understand these things. The study of wisdom exists in a totally different section. It does not exist in words. It exists within the cage of man's body. Only if we go deeper and deeper inside this cage will we understand. To be born as a transformed embryonic form within the cage, to go within that form, and then to see—this is what we must do as we proceed on and on. This does not exist in writings. We must realize this within. Amen.

# Three Questions

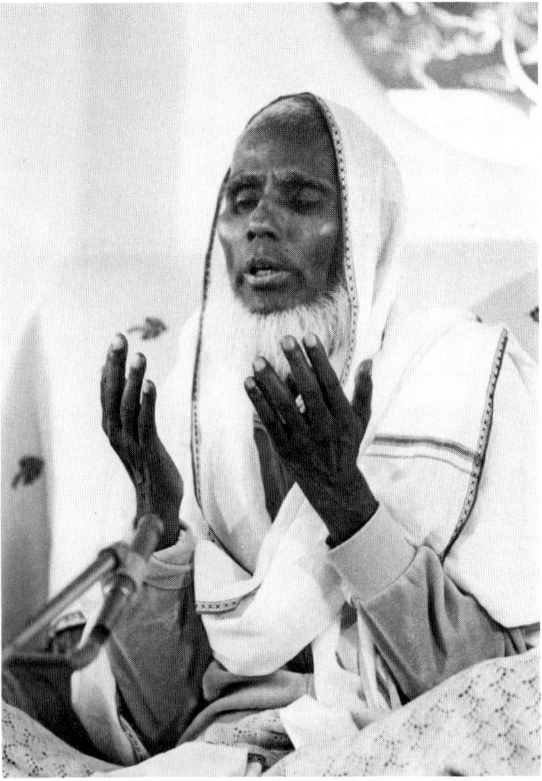

## HOW WILL I SEE YOU?

Where was I?
Allah, where was I before?
Where was I?
What place have I come to?
What will I do here?
Where did I live before?
Allah, where am I?
What must I do now?

How will I see You in this world?
Where are You?
Where are You?
In what place will I see You,
    O God, O Allah?
Will I see You in the world?
Will I see You in the body?
Will I see You in the next world?
Will I see You in my wisdom?
Will I know You and see You in all lives?

Who created me?
Who sent me down and placed me here?
Who made me of earth?
Who dwells hidden within me,
Causing me to do everything I do?
Who, Allāhu, who?

How will I know?
How will I understand You?
And where will I reach You?

October 23, 1979
Philadelphia, PA

My Brother,

May all praise and praising be to God. May God protect you. Amen. May your love and service to the world be dedicated to God alone. Amen. May God open the path for your life and your endeavors in serving the world. Amen. And to the secretary who works with you, may God bestow His bounteous grace, His wisdom, and His gracious qualities upon her life and her qualities. Amen.

My brother, you have traveled around the world and met many different people. You have talked to them, asked them many different questions, and listened to their answers. Some of the answers may have been helpful and others not so helpful; however, it gladdened our hearts to see the patience and tolerance with which you listened to all the answers. These qualities are precious gifts God has bestowed upon you, and we praise God for that.

Your experiential research and learning from these visits certainly appear meaningful. However, we must remember that there is One Power who knows everything, the Power that created all the universes, protects them, and causes them to move. May that Power protect you. Amen.

My precious brother, when seen through wisdom this world called creation is in reality a tiny atom. But the camera of ignorance blows it up, making it gigantic. The people of the world look at that picture, perceive it to be enormous, and roam and wander around and around in it. Since it is a world of dreams, there is no end to their wanderings. They go on dreaming the dream of their lives endlessly. This is the world.

Your research searches for a truth. You must have an awareness of that truth, otherwise you would not have embarked on this venture. What is called truth cannot be found in religions, races, or languages. Truth explains as wisdom within wisdom, as the inner being within the self, and as the meaning within the explanation. You would not have been asking these questions if you did not have some awareness of that truth.

I am a student learning from the creations of the world. Though advanced in years, I have not yet completed learning. From every creation I learn what they have to teach me. And if they ask, or if they are prepared to listen, I in turn tell them what I have learned. In the world I am a tiny student, as tiny as an ant, and until I come to fully know myself and understand the truth I will continue to learn as a student, tinier than the smallest ant.

I am presently residing in Philadelphia. On three occasions the children of this fellowship put your television programs on for me. I saw and listened to them with great interest. On one of the programs you mentioned that you had been asking three questions for the last thirty years and that no one had yet given you a satisfactory answer. The questions were, "Who am I? Why am I here? And who is God?"

This must certainly be a heavy burden if it has been weighing on your heart for as long as thirty years. I am a small man, but I have been asking the same questions for a long time. I feel I should share a little of what I have learned in the course of my travels, and in return, learn from you what you have understood.

Therefore, I am enclosing a letter containing some of what I have learned in the course of my experiences. I earnestly request you to read this letter from beginning to end. I do not know whether you will agree with it or not. If you do not agree, I will be most grateful if you will tell me what you know and what you have learned in your life. I ask this of you in all humility.

Although I am older than you, I have not had any education. You have more learning and more wisdom; one who has wisdom is really the older one. Therefore, although I am older in age, I make this request of you. My brother, please find the time to read through what is written and let us know what you have to tell us.

> All the dancing,
> All the singing,
> One man's becoming a slave to another,
> All the wandering and all the accumulation of wealth
> Is merely for the sake of the one-span stomach.

My dear brother, the dancing and the singing are the 64 arts of the sensual pleasures. Making the world one's own, attempting to rule the world, earning money by becoming slaves to one another, and wandering from country to country to amass wealth is done for the sake of filling the one-span stomach. But if one is assailed by hunger, the ten commandments will fly away.

If we understand this then we will know that there is—

One for meditation,
Two for propagation,
And four for burial.

To meditate, there can only be One. Only God can meditate on God; there cannot be two. A man must transform himself into God's state and become one with God before he can meditate.

For propagating the world, two are required, a male and a female, an Adam and an Eve. For a burial four people must carry the coffin. This is the way of the world. My brother, whether people fly in the sky or walk on the earth, this is their state in the world.

One who understands the state of meditation and cuts away his wandering and dancing in the world will burn away the joys and the sorrows known as hell. He will die within God and understand that God is the only One who can meditate on God.

This, my brother, is what a man needs to

know. This is what I feel, with the little wisdom I have. If there are any faults, please forgive me.

May God protect you, your loved ones, your parents, and those born with you. May God protect your secretary and her family. May He bestow the undiminishing wealth of His grace upon all of you. Amen.

*M. R. Bawa Muhaiyaddeen*

October 22, 1979

My brother,

On your television program you asked three questions: "Who am I? Why am I here? And who is God?" You said that for the past thirty years the religions of the world had been giving you answers, but that you have not been satisfied. This is because the world consists of outer speech and outer acts. The world does not understand and has not learned the answers to these questions. The world has not researched these questions.

My brother, you are a brother to all the religions which comprise the society of mankind. God created Adam (peace be upon him), and we are the family of Adam (A.S.). We are all one race. At the time Adam (A.S.) was created, six kinds of lives were placed within him: earth life, fire life, water life, air life, ether life, and human life, which is light life. In addition to these six kinds of life, God also placed within man true wisdom and its explanations: the explanations of the connection between man and God, of good and evil, right and wrong, heaven and hell, truth and falsehood, and countless other explanations.

Man has been formed as God's secret, and God is man's secret. The secret of man lies within God, and the secret of God lies within man. Man can and will try to know God, and God will know all the secrets of man, as man within God and God within man. It is in this state that God formed Adam (*A.S.*).

The various religious scriptures say that Adam (*A.S.*) was created out of earth and then placed in heaven. They say that satan ridiculed Adam (*A.S.*) out of pride and jealousy and spat his evil qualities upon him. As a result, the evil qualities of satan entered the body of man. Satan's destructive and divisive qualities and actions, the qualities of arrogant and envious thoughts, fights and wars, and the desire to attack and kill or destroy others spread throughout the body of man which had been created perfectly pure.

It is said that God then took Adam (*A.S.*) up to the world of heaven and created Eve (*A.S.*) to make a pair. Once again satan attempted to deceive Adam (*A.S.*) by making him eat the forbidden apple. As soon as Adam and Eve (*A.S.*) ate the apple, their beauty, their light, and their good qualities were ruined. They lost the eyes which could see God; now they could see only the world, hell, and illusion or *māya*. Instead of being aware of God, they began to be aware of certain disgusting aspects of their bodies. The light of God was concealed from them, and in its place they began to see the glittering darkness of hell. As a result, Adam and Eve (*A.S.*) were thrown out of heaven, along with satan. Later, when they realized their faults and begged forgiveness, God dispelled the darkness and returned their original beauty. This is what the scriptures say.

Because Adam (*A.S.*) lost his connection with God and took on a connection to hell and the qualities and actions of satan, mankind was separated from God. We were taken away from living in His company. From that point on, mankind multiplied. Man, satan, ghosts, and demons lived in the same world and in the same bodies. Men began to fight and have arrogance, jealousy, the pride of mine and yours, and religious and racial differences. The children of Adam (*A.S.*) separated, formed different languages, and developed the divisive qualities by which they would attack and kill one another.

The One who is called God has no form. He is

not any form man has made Him to be. God is not any of the gods man has made. He does not have the names man has given to Him. God is not a form, a shape, or a statue. God is One who is beyond all the divisiveness and discrimination of religion, philosophy, and doctrine. He has no birth or death. He has no blood-ties or selfishness. He has no hunger, disease, old age, or death. He is the power with the inherent ability to control all the energies or *saktis*, and all the elemental miracles or *siddhis* performed by creation.

Man is the ray of light which emerged from that power. The true form of man is light. The form which is man contains the capacity for perfect wisdom and the completeness of God's beauty and resplendence. There was a time when the ray known as man dwelled within the power which is God. But man left the light and came to the earth, because of his connections to and thoughts of satan, because of his love for earth, woman, gold, religions, and philosophies.

Man has come here to know himself and the power of God. All of creation is God's artwork. The creations reveal the grace of God, His artistry, and His work. Everything you see is a work of art created by God, and each explains His glory. God has said, "I have created so many trees, so many flowers, shrubs, birds, reptiles, crawling worms, insects, honeybees, cruel beasts, and lowly creations with various colors and hues. And I remain as the Ruler who protects them. O man, you have given up the connection to Me and left Me." These words were given to those who have wisdom and who have mingled with Him.

When man understands his connection with God, the world becomes a flower garden. When man understands himself and realizes who is his Chieftan, this world becomes a prayer mat. It becomes a prayer mat and a heaven. A man's heart is his world.

There are four different ways in which human beings, birds, and animals utilize this world. Some are actors and see it as a stage. Some see it as a school. Some see it as a flower garden and make their hearts into beautiful flowers. And some see it as a place for prayer and make their hearts into prayer mats.

To a man of wisdom, the world is a minute particle within a particle. If an atom were cut into ten million sections, the world would be as small to him as a tiny particle of one of those particles. If one particle is cut with his wisdom, and if he looks within it, he will see 99 particles which are God's miracles revolving one around the other without touching. If he takes one of those particles and cuts it with his divine luminous wisdom into 100,000 pieces, and if he then takes one of those pieces and cuts it open, again he will see 99 particles revolving one around the other without touching. That is God's *wilāyat*, His sovereign power.

If he takes one of those particles and cuts it into 50,000 pieces, and takes one piece of that and cuts it open, again he will see 99 particles revolving one around the other without touching. And if he takes one particle out of that and cuts it into 25,000 pieces and opens one of them, again he will see 99 particles revolving one around the other without touching. If he takes one of those particles and cuts it into 1,000 pieces and takes one of those pieces and cuts it open, again he will see 99 particles revolving one around the other without touching. If he takes one of those particles and cuts it into 500 pieces and takes one of those pieces and cuts it, again he will see 99 particles revolving one around the other without touching. And if he takes one of those particles and cuts it into 100 pieces and then cuts one of them, again he will see 99 particles revolving around and around without touching.

The power of God is displayed in its absolute totality within each of the 99 particles. And that power will draw wisdom into itself. That power is the *Nūr*, the complete resplendence of Allah. In the beginning man was a ray and that ray is pulled back into the power. The ray known as man which emerged from the power is drawn back into it. This is the power which we naturally and instinctively call God, even though we may speak of Him in many ways in many languages.

Man is light. Of the six kinds of lives, the true form of man is an exalted ray of light, the light form of his soul. The form of the soul cannot be seen or known by science. The form of light was placed within the cage of this body, which is like a shirt made of the five elements, the five kinds of lives. God formed the house out of the five kinds of lives and made it into a school for man to learn the secrets of God. God has told mankind, "This is a school in which to understand yourself and Me." Man was formed of earth, and he has come to the earth in order to learn about himself and the power which is the Father who created him.

The 18,000 universes, the 15 realms, and the physical world, all exist within the heart of man. One's world is his own heart or mind. One's mind is either the world of heaven or the world of hell. That is a great secret. There is the *sirr* and the *sifāt*. *Sirr* is the secret which must be seen within, and *sifāt* is what is seen outside as form. All the things which are created in manifest form are the *sifāt*. But that which was never created and which has no form is God. And when that which has no form merges with that which has form, that is man.

There is something that has no appearance; that is God's essence and grace, which is called His *dhāt*. When the light form of the soul sees and understands that grace and goes into that grace, that is true man, or Man-God. Then man is God, and God is man. The man who keeps the connection to God remains a true man with the resplendence, the connection, the beauty, and the power of God. He remains the ray which is always intermingled within that power.

Because man has come to this world to understand the story of the Father who rules the world, he has to understand the difference between God and satan, between hell and heaven. The human body is a vast university where man must learn these differences. This body is heaven, it is hell, it is divine wisdom, and it is illusion, or *māya*. It is God and it is darkness. Everything exists within this school. Man's life is a school, a university. Man has come here to study in this university in order to understand himself. Man must attain excellence in the examinations, and then go back to his Father, back to His kingdom where he came from originally.

Man has come here to learn his story, his Father's story, and about the artistic work of his Father—about the sun, moon, stars, sky, seas, lands, mountains, the nether worlds, the higher worlds, the seven worlds below, and the seven worlds above.

The world is man's heart, the central state between the seven heavens above and the seven hells below. The 18,000 universes exist within man's heart. All the fighting, wars, divisiveness, discrimination, theft, murder, falsehood, treachery, deceit, satan, animals, monkeys, elephants, cats, blood-sucking demons, creations with human faces, creations with satanic faces, man, the light, and God dwell in this world. Man has come to this university to study this world, to learn about the Father who is God, and to understand the explanation of the history of God.

Whatever man sees within himself is the world. Whatever man desires is hell. Whatever he praises or takes pride in becomes the instrument which will eventually kill him. He has come here in order to learn this. But some have come here as actors and dancers. All the dancers and actors want to act on the stage of the world in hope of winning prizes. Everyone wants to win prizes. Some want the prize of a heavenly kingdom. Some want political prizes. Some want religious prizes. Some want philosophical prizes. Some want to win titles as prizes, women as prizes, or gold as prizes. Some want to win the prizes of racial differences, the prizes of fame and position, or the prizes of learning and education. Some act for the sake of heaven, some for the sake of hell, and some to become kings. There are many millions of kinds of acting. These are the acts of the mind.

There are many, many actors who hope to receive prizes from God, but before the power called God gives the prizes, He will say, "All the actors who wish to receive a prize from Me, display your acts and then come forward to receive your prizes."

And everyone will begin to fight, saying, "My act is best. My song is best." Even though they are trying to win prizes from God, they fight with each other and break each other's heads. What God would have enjoyed watching, they have turned into a battlefield. They are destroyed in the world of the illusion of the mind and in the joys of desire which is hell.

A man of wisdom must think, "Where am I now? What am I doing? Where was I before? What was the reason for my coming here? Where will I go after this? Who am I?" The purpose of his life will be to learn the answers to these secrets. If man understands the answers to these questions, he will see the essence or *dhāt* and the manifestations or *sifāt*. Everything visible is the created external form, the *sifāt*. The *dhāt* was never created. That essence is the power which makes everything move. "What is that power? Who am I? Who am I in relation to that power?" Man must understand the answers to these questions. And to understand this, man must realize that everything which can be seen contains His story— the sun, the moon, the stars, and all the *sifāt* of God. No matter what man sees, he must split it open with his wisdom and look within. His learning is to open and look into all the creations of God.

If man examines and understands how the honeybee imbibes the nectar from the depths of a flower, he will wonder at the subtle nose with which the bee discovers the scent of the far-away nectar. The lotus which lives in the middle of a pond contains sweet honey, but that is not recognized by any of the fish, insects, frogs, or animals which live in and near the pond. The honeybee comes from far away, identifies, discovers, and imbibes this sweet honey. When we realize the subtlety with which God has created the honeybee, we will marvel and say, "My God, what a wonder! What a wonder Your art is. How beautiful is Your creation." A wise man will reflect on this, understand, and praise God.

Into a small seed, God has placed a huge tree with many branches, limitless numbers of leaves, and countless numbers of flowers. And He has made the trees bear many, many fruits. As man tastes each fruit, he exclaims, "My God!" He will understand that God has placed great secrets in such small seeds. He will open the fruit, understand, and then praise God, saying, "My God! What a wonder!"

Inside the seed he sees the tree, the branches, the leaves, the flowers, and the fruits. He sees the subtly shimmering leaves. "What a wonder, O God! See how each one of these millions of leaves dance and dance and praise You! Whether they are beaten by the winds or the gales, they trust You and they praise You with their movement. They move up and down worshipping You. With one seed, You created millions. From that tree came millions of fruits, all with identical tastes. The seed grew into a tree which bore the same kind of seeds. O God, You give back manifold the seed which earlier was destroyed in the earth and grew into a tree. You have made one into many. What a wonder!"

Look at the flowers God has made. He has created so many colors and hues. Inside the flowers, He has made a fragrance. And within the fragrace, right in the center, He has made a sweet honey. Was there any honey in the flower's seed? No. But the flower has honey.

No matter how much art work we do, all our work only imitates what we have seen. We examine something and draw a mechanical. We see a building and make another one. We read religious scriptures and then discourse on them. We learn something and write a history about it. One man writes something, the next man reads it. One man draws the blueprint, another man builds accordingly. One man says something, another man copies it. This is what we have been studying in the world. But we need to open all these things and look within them.

The first step is to think of God, the second is to understand, the third is to praise Him and see Him through that understanding, saying, "My God, what a wonder Your creation is!"

Each one of God's creations depicts His story. And when we understand His story, we will find and understand our story. When we have understood, we will have the thought and certitude of prayer. When we praise Him, it is His story. We will be able to understand the history of creation, our history, and God's history.

God has placed everything within man, including the wisdom by which we can see what has been revealed in His creation and praise

Him. He has placed within man the wisdom with which to see Him and the devotion with which to praise and glorify Him. All three things exist together: (1) knowing oneself, (2) understanding with wisdom, and (3) praising God, having realized Him in everything seen.

All of creation is a show with many scenes. Each scene depicts the story of the One who dwells within. When we understand that and see our story within, we will have the remembrance of Him and that will be our prayer. When we praise that, it is His story.

No matter what we look at, if we open it, we can see God and His grace. For example, we will realize that the light of the sun does not originate from the sun, but from the power which is God. In this way as we open each thing and look within, we will understand ourselves, realize Him, and praise Him. It is for these three things that we have come here.

Look at an ant. If a grain of sugar or a cake crumb has fallen somewhere, the ant can detect it even though we cannot. Even though our eyes cannot see it, the ant has the ability to find it and take it away. Amidst all the opposition it faces in this world, the ant finds its food, does it not?

See how it discovers its food through its sense of smell. Just as the ant disregards everything else to find sweetness, in the same way, no matter how many different scenes and shows exist in this world, no matter how many kinds of food there are in this world, no matter how many sections there are in this world, if man could disregard all of them and find God, if he could become a true man, wisdom would dawn within him. Then he could discover what his point is and what God's point is. He could discover the story of God living within man, he could learn his own story, the story of His Father, and the story of prayer.

It is man who makes his heart a heaven or hell. It is man who lives as satan, a ghost, a demon, or God. They are all within him. Man is the cause of destruction or goodness. It is man who looks at the world through divisiveness.

God created this world as a flower garden and placed so many different colors within it—black, white, yellow, and brown. Having created all the different colors, He looks at that flower garden which is so beautiful and is happy to see the many different colors in the same garden. He sees the colors and the fragrances which come from each flower. That is His artistry. It is to enjoy this art, these colors and fragrances, that we have come to this world. God enjoys seeing all the different colors with all their different fragrances living as one in the garden.

Man may be living in the east, west, north, or south, and he has many different languages and colors. God created man like the many different colored flowers in the garden and wanted these men to live in unity. He poured the water of His grace onto them to make all of them live in unity as one race and one family. He is happy when men live in unity. So many different fragrances, so many colors, and such beauty! This is what God enjoys.

When we paint something, we, too, use many colors, and it is beautiful. This is the way in which God has created mankind in this world—to be beautiful. Different colors joining together to live as one, to live in unity in the flower garden of the kingdom of God, to be the beauty of His truth, so that God can be blissful upon seeing the beauty of their unity. God has made man, the flowers, the trees, and all creations in this way. He has created birds and snakes with many different colors to bring beauty to the eye, so many different colors in unity.

Man, too, is a creation of God. His body of the five elements is a creation. But the soul, the ray of light which is truly man, came from God. Man must reflect on this. What makes God happy? Compassion, love, the unity of one family, the realization that there is only one God, and the realization that mankind is one race and that we are all one life. Nothing else is important other than knowing this, understanding this, seeing our Father, and joining with Him. There is nothing else.

God's happiness is true happiness. His compassion and His unity are complete. If one develops that completeness within his innermost heart, filling his heart with God when he looks at this world, that is the completeness which God praises. God accepts that heart.

But saying, "My race, your race. My religion, your religion. I am great and you are small," dividing one man from another, dividing one religion from another, one race from another, and one color from another, worshiping for the sake of heaven or hell, worshiping for the sake of elemental miracles or *siddhis* and occult powers, and worshiping for the sake of 'I' and 'you'—these are the qualities of satan, animals, demons, and ghosts. These are the hellboards, the billboards to hell. Man accepts these advertisements to hell and is taken in by the hellboard business. One who desires what is in these advertisements will be shown the path to hell.

Man must understand the answer to the question, "Who is God?" The answer is: God is a power which dwells within all lives. He is intermingled within all lives; He is to be seen within everything which can be seen. When we realize this we will see God within every creation. Once we have the wisdom to know this, we will have the wisdom which understands God, see Him, and praise Him.

There are three duties for which we have come to this world: to understand ourselves, to know Him, and to praise that power. These duties must be done just as a gem must be cut and faceted in order for the light to be revealed, just as sand must be refined in order to be made into glass. Just as current is extracted from water, man can see his true form if he can separate the currents of his evil qualities and actions from himself. As he separates himself from the five elements, he will begin to see his soul. When he sees his soul, he will understand himself. And when he understands himself, he will see his Father. This is the explanation of man's coming to this world. And when man understands this, he will go back to the house in which he dwelt earlier—the house of God, his Father. When he returns to his Father's house, he will do the work of his Father, he will rule in the kingdom of his Father, and he will receive the exaltedness of his Father. One who understands this and sees his Father finds that his story and the story of his Father are one. He is not destructible and his Father is not destructible. A man of wisdom must realize this.

Scientists have said that man evolved from a monkey. However, the body of man was conceived not from a monkey itself, but by monkey tricks. His body was born from monkey tricks. His mind and desire were born from arrogance, karma, and *māya*. But the true form of man was born from wisdom, completeness, and the briliant ray of God's light. When a man realizes and understands, he will know his story, God's story, and what he must learn in this school. Everything will point toward the path to his Father.

Even though there are four hundred trillion, ten thousand kinds of spiritual things, spiritual *saktis* and the miracles of animals are not what we need to see. The connection between God's miracle and man's miracle is good qualities, good actions, good conduct, non-attached and selfless duty, the quality of loving all lives as one's own life, the quality of disregarding the feeling of one's own hunger and feeling the hunger of others, disregarding one's own comfort and comforting all other lives as brothers and sisters. Our duty is to understand ourselves, to understand others, and to understand our Father.

We have come to this school to learn our duty. We have come here to learn the story of Adam (peace be upon him), the story of mankind and of all creation, to study all the art work of our Father, and to learn of the power which is the grace of our Father. This is what we must understand. This learning cannot be found in books, in religions, or in philosophies. This story can be found only within the creations of the artistry of God. And the only way we can discover His secret within each creation is to pay obeisance to Him by conducting ourselves with His wisdom, qualities, and actions.

Only through God can man know God's state. Only through God can man know the soul which belongs to Him. Only through God can man become peaceful.

Mankind, born so rare, came to this world to understand God and His qualities and actions. For those who were separated from their original state, God sent 124,000 prophets, His eternal devotees, as witnesses to prove the connection between man and God. Twenty-five of them were chosen as the clear witnesses. Of these, there were eight major prophets—Adam, Noah, Abraham, Ishmael, Moses, David, Jesus, and Muhammad (may God's peace and blessings be upon him and all of them). They were chosen as the clear witnesses who came to caution mankind and to bear witness to the connection between man and God.

All the prophets were sent by the same God to give step-by-step explanations. Each prophet came in each time to prove the existence of One God. They did not come to create different religions, different philosophies, or to cause division and separation among men. They came to witness the existence of God, not to say, "My race, your race. My religion, your religion. My God, your God. I will go to heaven, you will go to hell. We are the only ones who can go to heaven and all the others will go to hell." This is not what they came for.

They all came to witness the existence of One God. They came as witnesses for the children of Adam (peace be upon him), for men of divine analytic wisdom, and for men who have fallen because they have been deceived by satan. They came for those who created forms and statues and for those who made stones, bones, animals, snakes, scorpions, elephants, cows, and horses into gods; for those who made rats, fish, foxes, and dogs into gods; for those who made ghosts, demons, and spirits into forms and worshiped them as gods; and for those who made the thoughts of their minds and their qualities into gods. God told the prophets, "Go tell them these things are not God. There is only one God, and He is not any of these forms." He is a great Power. He is our Eternal Father. He is a resplendent light which Moses (peace be upon him) called Yahweh. Everyone calls God by a different name according to his own language, but God is

One. Though they use many different names, everyone speaks of the same God.

God is not One who gives heaven to some religions and hell to others. Heaven and hell exist according to each person's intention, searching, and goals. One who realizes the Lord, His Father, one who understands within his heart and then makes his heart a heaven, one who builds within his heart, one who speaks with his Father who is God, one who dedicates himself to his Father, and one who performs the actions of his Father receives heaven.

Heaven cannot be reached through religions. Religions go only as far as the cemetery. Religions cannot take us to God's kingdom. But one who understands the story of God's qualities, his own history, and God's history will have found a path to his Father. That is the connection and the path. If he sees God within himself and if he can conduct his life within God, then at the point where the two become one, he has attained the kingdom of heaven. What is called the kingdom of heaven is to contain the actions and the qualities of God within oneself. One who has built those qualities within himself has built heaven within himself. That is the kingdom of God, that is heaven, that is divine wisdom, and that is true prayer. That is the form of God. We must understand this.

This is what man has come to learn and understand. If man succeeds in understanding this, then heaven, the kingdom of God, and God will be seen inside. Then when man dies, only the power of God remains; as soon as the ray is absorbed only the power exists. There is no coming or going. Where can it go and where can it come from? It does not leave; therefore, it does not come back. Then the power is contained within the power, resplending as the power which is God. Then there is no heaven or hell. Only the beauty of the compassion of God and the undiminishing power of God are there. Everything in all the universes is within Him.

Attaining God and reaching Him is heaven. The kingdom of God is God's qualities and actions. Good actions and good qualities are heaven. If a man can build that heavenly kingdom within himself he will never find fault with anything, he will never perceive anything as high or low, because he will realize that everything in God's kingdom contains the power and the point of God. And he will see God within the power.

One who sees God sees himself. One who sees himself knows the secret of God. One who realizes the secret of God sees God. We were within Him earlier, and now we have come here to learn about Him. This is the learning which will give us victory. Once we attain that victory, we will see the kingdom of God, and we will see God within the form of light. The university of this body will be replaced by the body of light and wisdom.

We have come here to learn about the creations, about God's secret, and about God's grace. We are the form of light. There are six kinds of lives and we are the form of light. We have come here to learn the *sirr*, the secret connection between ourselves and His power, to study our Father and the story of where we were before. Within this body, within this show, there is much we must learn. We have come here to learn, not to dance on this dramatic stage or to watch show after show. We have come here to open and look within everything and see our Father. Each thing that we enjoy or feel sorrow about must be opened, and we must see God within. That is the lesson we have come to learn.

I do not want to say much and I am only conveying the little that I know, my brother. I am one of small wisdom. This is all I know. You asked these three questions at the end of your program. I do not have much wisdom, but I think this is the path and that this is what we have to learn. Since you asked these questions, my heart and my wisdom told me to say this to you. Please forgive me. These words came to me. I do not know whether they are right or wrong. But this is what I believe and what I have learned.

I have said what my heart told me to say. Please forgive me if there are faults in it. I am a small student and I am learning. There are so many in this world who are greatly learned. I am a lowly student with little learning, but I told you what I was told to say. If there are any faults, please forgive me. Amen.

My brother, in your program you also made another point. You said that doubt is necessary for the development of faith. There is a point in that. As long as gold remains buried inside the earth, there is doubt. But once it is taken out of the earth, once it has been polished and its true worth has been revealed, then the doubt ends. Once the true value of gold is recognized, then its place is different; it is no longer in the earth but in a treasury. Then there is no doubt.

As long as gold is inside the earth, many might come to dig and cut into the earth. The gold might think,"Who will cut here? Who will dig there? Will they harm me? Who will I go with? Will I be thrown in the trash? Will I be destroyed?" As long as the gold is inside the earth, it does not know these things. But once it is taken out of the earth and when its value is recognized, it will go to a treasury where it is appreciated and protected.

In this way, as long as one's faith is focused on love for earth, gold, and woman, it is as if it were buried in the earth, doubting and wondering,"Will I lose this? Will I lose that? Will this happen? Will that happen?" As long as we live trusting in heaven, miracles, and titles, then doubt will come because those are things which come and go. If we place our faith in changing things, we will have doubts. However, if man finds the One Treasure which does not change, in the place which does not change, if he places his faith in the Treasure which is eternally natural and original, there will no longer be any doubt.

In this world man thinks of *siddhis*, or elemental miracles. The world says if a man walks on water, it is a miracle. If a man flies in the sky, it is a miracle. If a man crawls into the earth unseen to others, it is a miracle. If a man jumps from one body to another, it is a miracle. If a man performs any of these 64 kinds of arts, they call it a miracle. If a man stands on his head, they call it a miracle. If he sits on the ground and lifts his backside a little bit off the earth, they call it levitation and say it is a miracle.

Look at the snake when it raises it's hood. See how high it rises from the earth. Is that a miracle? Look at the fish. They walk on water, they somersault, they swim to the depths and climb to the surface, and they sleep in the water. They do these things inside the water from the time they are born. If a tiny fish can do all this, can you call it a miracle if a man walks on water? Look at mosquitoes, honeybees, poisonous insects, and birds—all of them fly. An eagle can stand balanced and poised in the sky. A vulture flies in the sky and searches for distant carcasses to eat. If winged creatures can fly high in the sky, is it such a miracle when man flies? Walking on fire—is that a miracle? Some lives such as viruses and germs live in fire.

Look at the air. All the winds blow in the sky; they come and beat on man, on all the pores of his skin. In this way, how many different thoughts creep into man's mind, how many atoms creep into man's body, how many evils creep into man. Is this a miracle? Air creeps in through the pores of the skin. Even spirits creep into a man's body, satan comes into a man's body, many kinds of demons creep into man's body. They creep inside and work inside man's body. Is this a miracle? No. Mental forces, magic, and mesmerisms are not miracles.

Similarly, there are the worms, beetles, insects, and earth lives hidden in the earth. They are not miracles. You might find oil and water emerging from the same well. Oil burns and water is used to extinguish fire, but both exist in one place. Are these miracles? No. When man performs similar acts, are they miracles? Each of these are the natural actions of creations, acts which tiny atoms, cells, and viruses can do.

Man's duty is to ask questions similar to those you asked: "Who am I? Who is God? Why have I come here?" If after asking these questions man can understand his story and the story of God and praise God, if he can discover the unity between man and God, then that is the miracle. God's miracle is to make all lives bow in homage to Him. No life has seen Him, but through His cautioning, through the conscience, and the power which makes us say, "My God!" in times of danger, all lives bow to Him.

If man's qualities can become God's qualities, if that light, that truth, and that power can develop within a man, then all lives will revere him. Such a person will be like a flower blooming and becoming fragrant. The flower doesn't have to tell anyone of its fragrance; everyone who goes by experiences it. In the same way, if we learn what we came here to learn, that fragrance will develop within us. As soon as the fragrance of God manifests within us, the beings dwelling in the world will recognize that fragrance. They will discover it, and they will want to smell the sweet scent. When honey springs within the flower of the heart and the fragrance emerges, all lives will be able to smell and to recognize that fragrance. This is what God does. His fragrance, His sweet scent, and His qualities cause Him to be worshiped. This is His miracle.

He has displayed His art, and within it He

has placed the meanings. He has shown us the lessons we must learn; as soon as the understanding of that learning comes into us, the honey and the fragrance will come into us. Until we know that point, we will doubt; we will continue to doubt our faith. But the moment we understand, there is no doubt, because then there is only one point. There is only one point within His power. If we understand that one point, then doubt no longer exists.

Just as a seed perishes when the plant grows, we must perish so that the seed of the ray of light which dawned at the beginning can grow. And just as the plant then bears new seeds, that ray must return to its source as a new seed. When we reach that place, doubt disappears. Until then, doubt will persist.

All the changing creations and the changing things in which we place our trust create doubt— earth, religion, castes, colors, gold, silver, heaven, color stories, race stories, millions of deities, and millions of books. When everything we desire is subject to change, and when they do change, we doubt. We praise something and when it changes, we doubt. But when wisdom dawns, when faith emerges from that wisdom, and when we place our faith in the treasure that never changes, then there is no longer any doubt.

If there are any faults in what I have said, please forgive me. I am a small student in this world; I am still learning. I am learning a tiny amount of wisdom.

If a child wants to say something, the child will tell his father what is in his thoughts. In this way, we find we must tell you this. You must listen like the father listens to his child. It may be right or it may be wrong. If it is right, that is good. If it is not right, please tell us what is. A child must be taught. That is duty. Amen.

My brother, let us reflect on just a few more points. Cows and goats eat only shrubs, weeds, and grasses. Does that mean they have attained wisdom? No. Elephants eat fruits, leaves, shrubs, and grasses. Does that mean they have attained wisdom? Horses eat hay, some birds eat only fruits. Does that mean they have attained wisdom? Just because goats, cows, tiny birds, horses, and elephants do not eat any meat, do they attain wisdom automatically? No. The earthworm eats only earth, nothing else. Does that mean the earthworm has attained wisdom? Some creations live on air. Snakes eat various things, but they live on air for long periods of time. That does not mean the snake has attained wisdom.

Some worms, beetles, scorpions, snakes, and rats dwell inside little burrows. Have they attained wisdom through doing this? Some snakes live inside burrows for three and four months at a time without going out. Have they attained wisdom? A crane stands on one leg for eight to ten hours at a time just to catch one fish. It stands motionless on one leg to catch one fish. When people do yoga and perform mantras, does it mean they will attain wisdom? No. If a man avoids eating meat and fish and lives on grass, does he attain wisdom? The cows and goats end up in the butcher shop and the supermarket. Birds die or they are shot. They have not attained wisdom by not eating meat.

Just because someone chants mantras, performs *tantras* or tricks and meditations, does he attain wisdom? All these things lead only to the cemetery. The angel of death will come at the proper time and the man will have to die. Whether he is meditating in a cave or anywhere else, he has to die. Even if he flies in the sky, he must die. He will have to go to that supermarket called hell or the butcher shop in which he is torn apart by the snakes of hell, by the qualities he nourishes within himself. The very animals he nourishes within himself will tear him apart and eat the pieces. That state in not meditation.

My brother, true meditation is to understand the answers to the questions you have asked, to understand the self, to live without hurting or causing harm to or eating any other life. If we can acquire the qualities of God and search with wisdom for the answers, if we can really try to understand the self and understand our Chieftain, know Him, see Him, and praise Him, exclaiming, "My God," if that clarity comes, then that is true meditation, that is true prayer, that is true worship. That is the only prayer which will grant victory in our lives. Nothing else can grant this. That is real learning. That is what we have come here to learn. All the other things we think of as great achievements are being performed outwardly by the tiniest of creations.

The world is a school. We have come to the world in order to learn our story and God's story, to look at God's natural creations, to look at nature, and to study God. We have to open all things and look within. We have to open up religion and look within it. Religion is both a witness and a show, but we must open the religions and look at what is inside. It is when you look inside that the witness exists. God's witness is inside, and then we must look within the witness. There we will understand the proof of God's existence. And when we understand that proof, then our story will be within our understanding. The history of mankind is within that understanding, and if we understand that history, then we will understand what we came here to study. We will know what duties we have, we will know where we were before we came to the world, what duties we are doing now, and where we are going from here.

Religion is like a playhouse, and we must open that theater and look inside. We must open everything each religion has. We have to open each of the religions. If we open the religions and look inside, then we will see only one point, one family, one God, and one truth. God's story, the story of mankind, and the point of truth will be inside. There will be no discrimination, no differences, no separation, and no hell inside. There will be only one light inside. There is no darkness. The darkness is in the show. The questions, the answers, sounds, separations, and titles are all in the outer show. That state does not exist inside.

That is why the world is a school in which man must learn and understand. This is the reason we have come here. Please think of this. We must understand and learn. Wherever we are, that place is inside. And wherever we go, that story is inside. That story will appear in the place to which we will go from here, also.

Each of us who came here with wisdom must learn from this school. Heaven does not come from building beautiful churches, mosques, and temples. Man must build his church, mosque, and temple within himself. The house of God must be built within. The place of worship must be seen within. The completeness of God must be built within the self. If man can understand his story and the story of God and then build a church within himself, that is victory.

This victory is not accomplished through words, through dancing and acting, or by seeking titles, praise, or fame. When a man understands this, he will be rejected by the world.

When all the world rejects him, he will begin to inquire and learn. It is only when he leaves the dark room and comes out into the open space that he can learn. All the things a man desires must first reject him. It is only when all the things man has placed his trust in begin to reject him that he will come out and learn. That is his victory. Only then can he understand his history.

Who is God? Why am I here? And where will I go from here? These three questions will not be asked as long as blood-ties and relations and attachments to the world are holding on to us. We will not feel like asking these questions as long as those things hold us. Only when we are rejected by everything will we begin to ask, "Who am I? What is my story? What is God's story? What is the reason for my coming here?" Until then our possessions and attachments keep us in bondage, and we cannot learn. Until we are rejected, and until we come into the open and leave all the changing things, we can never learn, because our story will be the story of changing things.

My brother, all the prophets came and preached to the people. Buddha also came and preached to the human generation, telling them they must live in unity. Buddha, the son of Siddhartha, described the five precepts called the *pancha-sila*. These five precepts refer to the five elements which comprise man's body: earth, fire, water, air, and ether. The Buddha preached that we must do good to the bodies made of these five elements.

First of all, Buddha said that we must do our duty and help all those who have this body of man. He spoke about our charity, our duty in the world, about surrender, and about helping other lives. But Buddha did not speak about God. Why? Buddha was the only one at that time who was in communion with God. He was the only one who understood the meaning of the five precepts. He had escaped from the confinement of his body to the wide open space within from where he was meditating on God. But his meditation was meant only for a true man who had managed to escape from the things that kept him confined. Only such a man can meditate on God.

In order to know that state, first one has to transform oneself into a true human being. One has to become a true human being before he can understand God. This means he has to give up all the various states in which he exists, all his thoughts, his mind, and his desire, and all the things that the mind and desire cling to, his attachment to his relatives, to his religion, to his possessions and property. He must escape from all the things of the world and become free, unhampered and uncluttered like the soul when it emerged from God. It is only after he has given up everything and reached that state of freedom that we can talk to him about God.

Buddha was teaching the people how to become truly human. Because no one had become a human being, Buddha never mentioned God. It is impossible to talk about God to someone who cannot understand, someone who has not become free of all the things which hamper and veil him. This is why Buddha did not speak about God. Although he searched for a true human being until the time his state was to change and it was time for him to leave this world, although he saw many human forms, he never saw the qualities of a true man. He never found a real man. He saw that everyone in human form had a mixture of good and evil, and that these human beings were not trying to escape from what was veiling them and holding them down. This is the reason Buddha never spoke about God.

Buddha was meditating on God, but he never spoke to the people about God; they were worshiping the *pancha-sila*, the five precepts of the elements and of their society. They sought refuge in the society called the *sanga*, in the teachings or the *dharma*, and in the Buddha. In Tamil, *buddhu* means the idol of the human form. *Buddham saranam katchami* therefore means I surrender to this body. *Dharmam saranam katcham:* I surrender to the teachings and to charity and service toward mankind. *Sangam saranam katchami:* I surrender to the society.

Buddha could speak about God only when he found a human being who had given up everything in the world and had come out into the wide open space. Since he did not see anyone like that, he never mentioned God. Like this, only when man gives up everything, can one speak to him about God. Until mankind comes to that state, although we may see human forms and human faces in the world, they contain the qualities of so many animals. It is only when they come out into the open space and see themselves as true men that it becomes easy for us to speak to them about God; then it is easy for man to see God. Only when they reach that state can we explain to them the state of prayer and the state of merging with God.

In the same way, we cannot speak about God

to people who are not in that state. All the explanations being given are about things visible to our eyes. This is all they have been talking about. But we must see God with our wisdom, which is beyond what we can see with our eyes and our intellect.

Only when we have extracted our true self and become free can we realize ourselves, realize God, and realize the nature of our actions. Only then can we know what is yet to be done. Then we will know why we came here, who we are, and who God is. Then we can understand where we were before and where we are now. We must understand this in order to reach the state of a true man. As long as we do not realize this, we remain in the state of worshiping all the scenes and visions in the world. We must realize this.

Amen. May God protect you. May He bestow His limitless grace and undiminishing wealth upon you and your family, upon your secretary and her family. Amen. Amen.

# Glossary

(A) indicates an Arabic word. (T) indicates Tamil. (S) indicates Sanscrit.

*al-hamdu lillāh* (A)　All praise is to You. The glory and greatness that deserves praise is Allah. You are the One responsible for the appearance of all creations. Whatever appears, whatever perishes, whatever receives benefit or loss—all is Yours. I have surrendered everything into Your hands. I remain with hands outstretched, spread out, empty, and helpless. Whatever is happening and whatever is going to happen is all Yours. Lit.: All praise is to and of Allah!

*alif, lām, mīm* (A)　Three letters of the Arabic alphabet (ا ل م). In the transformed man of wisdom, these letters are represented as: *alif*—Allah; *lām*—*Nūr*, the light of wisdom; and *mīm*—Muhammad (*Sal.*).

*Allāh* (A)　God; the One who is beyond comparison or example; the eternal, effulgent One; the One of overpowering effulgence.

*Allāhu ta'ālā* (A)  God Almighty; God in the Highest. *Allāhu:* the beautiful undiminishing One. *Ta'ālā:* the One who exists in all lives in a state of humility and exaltedness.

*'arshul-mu'min* (A)  The throne of the true believer; the throne of one who has steadfast *īmān* [absolute faith, certitude, and determination]; the throne of an *insān* [true man] who has the perfect certitude of *īmān*. Allah will reside within the heart which praises Him and within the tongue which praises Him, the tongue which speaks only virtuous thoughts, the tongue which speaks the truth and praises the truth.

*As-salāmu 'alaikum wa rahmatullāhi wa barakātuhu kullahu* (A)  May the peace of God and His beneficence be upon all of you!

*Bismillāhir-Rahmānir-Rahīm* (A)  In the name of God, Most Merciful, Most Compassionate. *Bismillāh:* Allah is the first and the last. The One with the beginning, and the One without beginning. He is the One who is the cause for creation and for the absence of creation, the cause for the beginning and for the beginningless. *Ar-Rahmān:* He is the King. He is the Nourisher, the One who gives food. He is the Compassionate One. He is the One who protects the creations. He is the Beneficent One. *Ar-Rahīm:* He is the One who redeems; the One who protects from evil, who preserves and who confers eternal bliss; the Savior.

On the day of judgment and on the day of inquiry and on all days from the day of the beginning, He protects and brings His creations back to Himself.

*Dhikr* (A) The *wilāyats* [powers] of Allah and His grace have been praised in so many ways. *Dhikr* is a common name given to those words of praise. Out of those *Dhikrs*, the most exalted *Dhikr* is to say, "*Lā ilāha ill-Allāhu*—Other than You there is no God. Only You are Allah." That is the most exalted *Dhikr*. All the others relate to His *wilāyats* or His actions, but this *Dhikr* points to Him and to Him alone.

*gnānam* (T) Divine analytic wisdom. Allah has placed within the body of man the wealth of all the 18,000 universes. Man holds within his hands: hell and heaven, good and evil [*khair* and *sharr*], the secret and the manifestations [*sirr* and *sifāt*], the essence and the manifestations [*Dhāt* and *sifāt*], and that which is forbidden and that which is permissible [*harām* and *halāl*]. Allah has placed within him the wealth of the world, of heaven and hell; the wealth of the base desires [*nafs*]; the wealth of satan; the wealth which desires desire; the treasure which earth desires, which water desires, which fire desires, or which the air and the spirits desire; and the treasures which illusion [*māya*] desires. If man can discard all these treasures and take within him only the treasure called Allah and His qualities and actions, His conduct and behavior, if he makes Allah his only treasure and completeness, that is the state of *gnānam*.

What treasure is there other than Allah? All the rest is *agnānam* [ignorance] and *poignānam* [false wisdom]. *Agnānam* is the *gnānam* of the world. False wisdom is the *gnānam* of darkness, the speech which one speaks in the torpor and intoxication of darkness. *Agnānam* is the speech from the intellect; *vingnānam* [scientific wisdom] is the explanation given by the subtle intellect. *Meignānam* is to know and understand. *Meignānam* is from Allah's words; it is to know and understand through those words and to eliminate all that is evil. Other than Him there is no treasure. To know that everything other than Him is perishable and destructible and to throw them away—that is *meignānam*.

*hayāt* (A)  The plenitude of man's life; the splendor of the completeness of life; the *rūh*, or the soul of the splendor of man's life.

*'ilm* (A)  Divine knowledge; the ocean of knowledge; the ocean of grace.

*imān* (A)  Absolute, complete and unshakable faith, certitude, and determination that God alone exists; the complete acceptance of the heart that God is One.

*Īmān-Islām* (A)  The state of the spotlessly pure heart which contains Allah's Holy Qur'an, His divine radiance, His divine wisdom, His truth, His prophets, His angels, and His laws. The pure heart which having cut away all evil, takes on the power of that courageous determination called faith and stands shining in the resplendence of Allah.

When the resplendence of Allah is seen as completeness within the heart of man, that is *Īmān-Islām*. When the complete unshakable faith of the heart is directed toward the One who is completeness; when that completeness is made to merge with the One who is completeness; when that heart communes with the One who is completeness, trusts only in Him, and worships Him, accepting only Him and nothing else, accepting Him as the only perfection and the only One worthy of worship—that is *Īmān-Islām*.

*insān* (A)  True man; a true human being; the true form of man; the form of Allah's qualities, actions, conduct, behavior, and virtues. The one who has the completeness of this form, who has filled himself with these qualities—he is an *insān*.

*Insān Kāmil* (A)  A perfected, God-realized being. One who has made Allah his only wealth, having cut away the wealth of the world and the wealth sought by the mind. One who has acquired God's qualities, performs his action accordingly, and contains himself within those qualities.

*Islām* (A)  Spotless purity; the state of absolute purity. To accept the commands of God, His qualities, and His actions, to establish that state within oneself, and to worship Him alone. To cut away the desire called *'ishq*, to accept Him and know Him without the slightest doubt, and then to worship Him is Islam. To accept *Lā ilāha ill Allāhu* [There is nothing other than You, Only You are God] with certitude, to strengthen one's *imān* [absolute faith, certitude, and determination], and to affirm this *Kalimah*—that is the state of Islam. Also: the religion or creed of Islam.

*kalai gnānam* (T)   The wisdom of the 64 arts and sciences. These include the arts of making statues, idols and forms; circus tricks, dancing, playing games, physical exercise, yoga, all the drama and the acting; all the things we see with our eyes and the things we see with our mind; and the sciences such as making engines, planes, motors, and cycles.

Whatever arts man creates merely imitate or copy something he has seen. Acting out what he has studied and acting out all the four hundred trillion, ten thousand kinds of occult powers and mantras, acting out all these is collectively referred to as *kalai gnānam*.

Prayer to idols and statues and prayer to earth and water arise from these *kalais*. This is the *gnānam* [wisdom] that relates to form or creation. This is a branch of *agnānam* [false wisdom]. *Meignānam* [true wisdom] refers to the prayer which knows Allah alone, prayer which knows no equal.

*kalam* (T)  Time, which is comprised of arrogance, karma and illusion [*māya*]. Not to be confused with the Arabic word *qalam* which means 'the pen'.

*Kālan* (T)  The Angel of Death.

*khair* (A)  That which is right or good, as opposed to *sharr* [evil or bad]; that which is acceptable to wisdom and to Allah.

*Lā ilāha ill-Allāhu* (A)  There is nothing other than You, Only You are God. There are two aspects. *Lā ilāha* is the manifestation of creation [*sifāt*]. *Ill-Allāhu* is the essence [*Dhāt*]. All that has appeared, all creation, belongs to *lā ilāha*. The One who created all that, His name is *Allāhu*. "Other than You there is no God. Only You are Allah." To accept this with certitude, to strengthen one's *īmān* [absolute faith, certitude, and determination], and to affirm this *Kalimah*—this is the state of Islam.

*lām* (A)  The Arabic letter ( ل ) which correlates to the English consonant 'L'. In the transformed man of wisdom, *lām* represents the *Nūr* [the resplendence of Allah]. See also: *alif*.

*mīm* (A)  The Arabic letter ( م ) which correlates to the English consonant 'm'. In the transformed man of wisdom, *mīm* represents Muhammad. The shape of *mīm* is like a sperm cell and from this comes the *nuqat*, or dot, which is the form of the world. See also: *alif*.

*Muhammad* (A)  The effulgent face of God's light; The brilliant heart of grace; the essence of God; the Messenger of Allah which emanates from Allah; the *Nūr* or effulgence of Allah; the beauty of God's qualities which entrances everything in creation.

There are three *mīms* in Muhammad, and one is this beauty. The common meaning for Muhammad is the last one of the line of prophets. But, in truth, Allah has said, "O Muhammad, I would not have created anything without you." That same beauty called *mīm* which came at the beginning also comes at the end as the beauty of Muhammad. If something was not there at the beginning, it can not come at the end.

*māya* (T)  Illusion; the unreality of the visible world; the glitters seen in the darkness of illusion; the 105 million glitters seen in the darkness of the mind which result in 105 million rebirths; an energy [*sakti*] that can take many, many millions of hypnotic forms.

If man tries to grasp these forms with his intellect, he will see a form but he will never be able to catch it, for it will take on yet a different form. *Māya* is an energy which takes on various shapes, makes man forfeit his wisdom, and confuses and hypnotizes him into a state of torpor.

*māya sakti* (T)   The energies or forces of illusion.

*mu'min* (A)   A true believer; one of true *īmān* [absolute faith, certitude and determination].

*Nūr* (A)   The resplendence of Allah; the plenitude of the light of Allah; the completeness of Allah's qualities. When the plenitude of all this becomes one and resplends as one, that is the *Nūr*, that is Allah's qualities and Allah's beauty.

*pancha sila* (S)   The five precepts or minimum moral obligations taught by Buddha: 1) not to destroy life, 2) not to steal, 3) not to commit adultery, 4) not to tell lies, 5) not to take intoxicants.

*pūjā* (T)   Ritual devotion. Performing *pūjā* is: the offering of worship to the thoughts and demons that arise in one's mind; making a form of the thoughts and demons of the mind and worshipping them within and without; and offering flowers, fruits, and various things to the deities of the mind. Because those deities live in darkness, people light candles for them and ask them to come out. Then they ask those deities to provide them with light. To manifest the forms from one's thoughts into idols and to worship them as deities is called *pūjā*.

*purānas* (T)   Hindu scriptures; mythologies, legends, epics. The stories of each religion can be described as *purānas*. One religion calls it the Bible, another calls it the Qur'an. Some stories were sent down as commandments from God, others were created through man's intellect and senses, while still others were created by poets, usually as songs of praise that tell a story.

*qalb* (A)  The heart within the heart of man; the inner heart. Bawa explains that there are two states for the *qalb* and four chambers. The four chambers are earth, fire, air, and water, representing Hinduism, Fire Worship, Christianity, and Islam. Inside these four chambers there is a flower, the flower of the *qalb*, which is the divine qualities of God. It is the flower of grace [*rahmat*]. His fragrance exists only in this *qalb*. The four chambers are black; they are really the dog [*kalb*], the black dog which is the world, the thought of the world and the five elements.

But Allah's truth and His fragrance is that flower of the heart. That is the kingdom of Allah's church or mosque. There are some who worship in the darkness and some who worship in the light. Those who worship within that flower worship in the light. One section is light and the other four sections are night.

*qudrat* (A)  The power of God's grace and the qualities that control all other forces.

*Qutb* (A)  Divine wisdom, divine analytic wisdom, the wisdom which explains; that which measures up sand and thread it into a rope, or he may turn flowers into precious stones. These are all *siddhis,* or occult powers.

The *siddhar* shows these various tricks, but they are just energies connected to the earth. They are formed from the earth, they eat the earth, they will perish in the earth, and they remanifest themselves from the earth.

Those who perform *siddhis* in the present day are called scientists. They fly in the sky, walk on water, and perform so many *siddhis* by using iron, earth, water, fire, oil, gas, chemicals, and by utilizing light and the sun and moon. Scientists utilize the same things that *siddhars* used in the past.

But if one is bewitched and fascinated by God instead of being fascinated and bewitched by this sort of thing, that person will not have wasted his time in this world. The best and rarest accomplishment of all is to control one's mind and to reach the state where one can know God.

*siddhi* (T) Magic; miracle; supernatural abilities, commonly called miracles, obtained by devotion to and control of the elements. This term may be used to mean a person capable of performing miracles. See also: *rishi.*

*sifāt* (A) The manifestation of creation; attributes; all that has come into appearance as form; that which arose from the word "*Kun!* [Be!]"

*sirr* (A) The mystery of God; His secret.

*surāt* (A) A chapter of the Qur'an. Spelled in Arabic with a different 's' it means form, shape, pictorial representation, illustration, figure, statue.

*tantra* (T) A trick; a cunning trick performed with the motive of self-praise or self-gain.

*tarahan, singhan, suran* (T) *Tarahan, singhan,* and *suran* are the three sons of *māya* [illusion]. The first son, *tarahan* is the force that passes through the birth canal or vagina. That is the force of the mind, or the arrogant force of the elephant. The thought of the sexual act, or the force of that thought, passes first through that canal. The second son is *singhan*, the quality of the lion, the arrogance present at the moment of conception when the semen is ejaculated. The third son is *suran*, the illusory body formed at the time of conception. *Suran* is the many millions of thoughts and forms, the many millions of ideas and emotions, and the four hundred trillion, ten thousand energies and qualities. These are all the forms of *māya*. They are the energies and *saktis* which take many millions of different forms and are constantly changing from one form to another.

These are the sons of *māya*. They will never die as long as earth, fire, water, air, ether, mind, and desire exist; they will continue to take form after form after form. Only if the five elements, mind, and desire die will these three die. Otherwise there is a never-ending battle, a battle between wisdom and the demonic qualities of *tarahan, singhan*, and *suran*. This battle goes on within everyone. It is a great and never-ending war that is fought within every man in order to vanquish and conquer these three. Only when wisdom conquers and destroys these three can we reach the state of divine analytic wisdom [*gnānam*].

*Tarahan, singhan*, and *suran*—these three go together; they cannot be divided. *Tarahan* is the quality of the elephant. That is karma, arrogance, and lust. *Singhan* is the quality of the lion, the force of the act. *Suran* is all the qualities and energies of the mind. These three must be destroyed. As soon as these are destroyed, *māya* will leave of its own accord; it will run away and hide.

These three are forced and impressed upon the fetus at the time of conception.

*wilāyat* (A)  God's power; that which has been revealed and manifested through God's actions; the miraculous names and actions of God; the powers of His attributes through which all creations came into existence.

*Yā Rabbal-'ālamīn* (A)  O Ruler of the universes! The creator who nourishes and protects all of His creations forever.

# Index

*Passim* denotes that the references are scattered throughout the pages indicated (e.g. 102-107 *passim*).

Abraham *(A.S.)*, 118
Actors in the world, 101, 106-107
Adam *(A.S.)*, 95, 97-99, 117-119 *passim*
*Ahad; see,* God, the One
*Alif,* 40-41
Animals, 43-47 *passim,* 58-85 *passim,* 125, 129-131, 137
Ant finds its food, 111-112
Apple trees, 33-35, 39
Atom, cut into particles, 101-103
Attachments, 134

Bawa Muhaiyaddeen *(Ral.),* as student, 92-96, 123, 129
Bee imbibes nectar, 108
Believer, true, 22-25
Benefits, each creation — another, 7-9, 11-12
Body, creations within, 16-20, 36-50, 99, 105-138 *passim*
*see also* Worlds, inner and outer
Books of God; *see* God, study the lessons of
Breath, remember God with every , 12-15
Buddha, 134-138
Burdens, give to God, 14-16

Chickens scratch for food, 43-47 *passim*
Colors in unity, 113-114
Comfort other lives, 8-9, 33-34
Conception, 68, 77-85
Conscience, 127
Creations in the world, 32-33, 57-85 *passim,* 100-101,

104-138 *passim*
Creations within the body; *see* Body, creations within

David *(A.S.)*, 118
Death, 130
Death, die before, 48, 95
*Dhāt; see* God, light of
*Dhikr,* 13
Divisiveness, 114-115
Doubt, 123-129 *passim*
Duties, three — to perform, 115-117, 135

Elements, five, 57-58, 64-65, 68, 82, 97, 103, 135
Embryo; *see* Conception
Energies; *see* Saktis
Essence; *see* God, light of
Eve *(A.S.)*, 95, 98-99

Faith, 123-124, 128-129
Faultfinding, 121
Flowers, 9-10, 61, 101, 109, 112-113, 127
Forms of creation; *see* Creations in the world
Freedom, 136-138 *passim*
Fruits, 33-35, 39, 61

Garden, flower; *see* Flowers

God,
  believe in, 59-60
  die within, 48, 95
  the Father, 105-106, 116-117, 120
  grace of, 13, 29-32 *passim*, 36, 44, 47, 54-55, 75, 78, 81, 100, 104, 111
  kingdom of, 80-83, 120-122
  light of, 31-32, 37-49, 100-104 *passim*, 122, 128
  the mystery of, 55-60 *passim*, 70-73, 81-83, 98, 122
  the One, 5-6, 11, 29-31, 41-42, 99-100, 118-120
  the power of, 74, 81, 92, 102-104, 107, 115, 121-122
  praise, 110-115 *passim*
  remember on every breath, 12-16
  son of, 78, 83-84
  study the lessons of, 76-85, 103-138 *passim*
  surrender to, 15-16
  the treasure, 39-42 *passim*, 53-54, 60, 75, 124
  witness of, 132
Gold, 123-124
Grace of God; *see* God, grace of

Heart, innermost, 9-10, 37-38, 58, 66-85 *passim,* 101, 104-105, 114, 120

Heaven, 37, 98-99, 101, 104-106, 120-121

Hell, 37, 69, 73, 75-76, 99, 104-107, 114-115, 120-121, 130-131

Honey bee imbibes nectar, 108

Human being, become a true, 18-27, 37-38, 44-50, 55-85, 100-138, *see also* Man-God

Hunger, 56-57

Idol worship, 62-85, *see also* Worship

Illusion, 39, 62-63 *passim,* 79-80, 105, 107

*Imān,* 13, 19-24 *passim,* 38, 47-49

Ishmael *(A.S.),* 118

Islam, 21-22, 24, 47

*Insān-Kāmil; see* Man-God

*Insān-Kāmil Sheikh; see* Sheikh, we need a,

Jesus *(A.S.),* 78

Judgment, pass — on oneself, 20-25

Justice, act with, 20-25

Karma, 63

Kingdom of God; *see* God, kingdom of

*Lā ilāha ill-Allāhu,* 14-15

*Lām,* 40-42

Learning of God; *see* God, study the lessons of

Leaves of a tree, 108-109

Lessons of God; *see* God, study the lessons of

Life, reach maturity in, 35-36

Light of God; *see* God, light of

Man, creations within; *see* Body, creations within

Man-God, 17, 55-56, 67-85, 98, 104, *see also* Human being, become a true

Man, light life of; *see* God, light of

Man, perfected; *see* Man-God

Man, true; *see* Human being, become a true

Mantras, 130

*Maya; see* Illusion

Meditation, 95, 130-131

*Mīm,* 40-41

Mind, 104

Miracles, 61-85, 125-127

Monkey, man evolved from, 116

Moses *(A.S.),* 118-119

163

Muhammad *(Sal.)*, 118
Mystery of man and God; *see* God, the mystery of
Noah *(A.S.)*, 118
*Nūr,* 18, 103

*Pancha-sila,* 134-137
Particles of an atom, 101-103
Prayer, 13, 25, 110-112, 121, 131, 137
Prayer mat, 101
Pretend to believe in the world, 56-59
Prizes given by God, 106-107
Prophets, 18-20, 36-49 *passim,* 118-119
*Puranas,* seventeen, 57-58, 73

Qualities, animal; *see* Animals
*Qutbiyat,* 18

*Rasūls,* 36-37
Rebirth, 35, 65-85
Rejection by the world, 133-134
Religions, 97, 120, 131-133

*Saktis,* 32, 61-85
Satan, 98-99, 119
School to learn secrets of God, 103-138
Secret of God and man; *see* God, the mystery of

Seed, 108-109, 128
Sheikh, we need a, 43-49
Shepherds to lives within the body, 18-20
Ship can carry heavy weights, 14-16
*Sifāt,* 104, 107, *see also* Creations
*Sirr,* 104, *see also* God, the mystery
Son of God; *see* God, son of
Soul of man, 38, 103-104, 114, 136
Stage, world as, 101, 106-107
Stomach, one-span, 94-95
Stories of God; *see* God, study the lessons of

Teacher, *see* Sheikh
Time, 54
Titles of the world, discard, 44-45
Treasure that is God; *see* God, the treasure
Trees, 7-8, 33-34, 61, 108-109
Truth, 92-93

'Umar 'ibnul-Khattāb, 20-21
Understand oneself, 103-138
Unity, 113-114
Universes, 18,000, 17, 76, 104-105
Universes within the body; *see*

Body, creations within
University; *see* School to learn secrets of God

Vegetarianism, 130
Victory of man, 133-134

Wealth, accumulating, 94
Weight, give — to God to carry, 14-16
*Wilāyat; see* God, the power of
Wisdom
   have animals attained —? 129-131
   look with, 63-85, 92, 97, 101-123 *passim*, 128-133, 138
   seven levels of, 17-18
Witness of God, 132
World
   rejection by the, 133-134
   within man; *see* Worlds, inner and outer
Worlds
   inner and outer, 57-85, 92-138 *passim*
   *see also* Body, creations within
   three, 75, 78
Worship, 13, 25, 74, *see also* Idol worship

Yahweh, 119

## Books by
## M. R. Bawa Muhaiyaddeen

*Truth & Light: brief explanations*

*Songs of God's Grace*

*The Divine Luminous Wisdom
That Dispels the Darkness*

*The Guidebook to the True Secret of the
Heart (Volumes One and Two)*

*God, His Prophets and His Children*

*Four Steps to Pure Iman*

*The Wisdom of Man*

*A Book of God's Love*

*My Love You My Children:
101 Stories for Children of All Ages*

*Come to the Secret Garden:
Sufi Tales of Wisdom*

*The Golden Words of a Sufi Sheikh*

*The Tasty, Economical Cookbook
(Volume Two)*

*Sheikh and Disciple*

*Maya Veeram or The Forces of Illusion*

*Asmā'ul-Husnā:
The 99 Beautiful Names of Allah*

*Islam and World Peace:
Explanations of a Sufi*

*A Mystical Journey*

*Questions of Life/Answers of Wisdom*

*Treasures of the Heart:
Sufi Stories for Young Children*

*Gems of Wisdom 1/
The Value of Good Qualities*

*Gems of Wisdom 2/
Beyond Mind and Desire*

*To Die Before Death:
The Sufi Way of Life*

For free catalog or book information call:
(215) 879-8604

The central branch of the Bawa Muhaiyaddeen Fellowship is located in Philadelphia, PA. The Fellowship serves as a meeting house and as a reservoir of people and materials for all who are interested in the teachings of Bawa Muhaiyaddeen.

For information, write or call:

The Bawa Muhaiyaddeen Fellowship
5820 Overbrook Avenue
Philadelphia, Pennsylvania 19131

Telephone: (215) 879-6300